PELICAN BOOKS
A 162
LOCAL GOVERNMENT IN
ENGLAND AND WALES
W. ERIC JACKSON

LOCAL
GOVERNMENT

IN ENGLAND AND WALES

BY

W. ERIC JACKSON

PENGUIN BOOKS

Penguin Books Ltd, Harmondsworth, Middlesex
U.S.A.: Penguin Books Inc., 3300 Clipper Mill Road, Baltimore 11, Md
AUSTRALIA: Penguin Books Pty Ltd, 762 Whitehorse Road,
Mitcham, Victoria

—

Published by Penguin Books 1945
Revised and reprinted 1949
Reprinted 1951, 1954
New edition 1959
Reprinted 1961

—

Made and printed in Great Britain
by Hunt, Barnard & Co. Ltd
Aylesbury

CONTENTS

Preface to New Edition, 1959   7

Introduction   9

1. What is Local Government, and Why?   13
2. Who are the Local Authorities?   39
3. The Constitution and Election of Local Government Authorities   60
4. What Local Authorities Do   85
5. How They Do It   119
6. Local Government Officials   146
7. Where does the Money Come From?   169
8. Supervision and Control over Local Authorities   193
9. Which Way is it all Going?   206

Index   219

PREFACE TO NEW EDITION, 1959

SINCE the first issue of this book in 1945, many changes in local government law have taken place by reason of the numerous Acts of Parliament passed since that date, particularly the Local Government Act, 1958. It is hoped that the present issue, fully revised and brought up to date will be as popular and serviceable as were the former issues.

INTRODUCTION

LOCAL government is the concern of everyone. Every man, woman, and child in this country is, at some time or other, intimately affected by the operations of local authorities. The indifference which (to judge from the percentages of votes cast at local government elections) is at times displayed by some citizens towards their local councils does not alter the fact that the degree of efficiency with which the local councils carry on their work can do much to make or mar the well-being of the public whom those councils exist to serve.

The work of local government affects us all from many directions. Why are there no more in this country any great plagues as there were in former times? Whose business is it to provide the local fire brigade? Who arranges for the schooling of by far the greater proportion of the child population of this country? When you go to a public entertainment and feel sure that the premises are safe, whose concern is to to see to that? Who attends to the cleaning and mending of the public roads? All these things done badly, or done well, affect the happiness of all of us.

These and many other matters form the work of local government. Local government is democratic. The local councils are elected by the people. The people therefore have it in their hands to guard their own interests in the working of the local services.

One reason, among others, for a certain lack of interest in this important branch of public affairs is the lack of popular literature on local government. It is a large and complex subject. The Acts of Parliament and the legal decisions on local government topics form a vast mass and cover a wide range. There are many books for the expert, great volumes which are in constant use by public officials and lawyers. There are many commendable manuals for the student who wishes to qualify for appointment in the local government service. All these books would fill many shelves. The standard works on such matters as public health, education, rating and valuation, highways, water-supply, and elections run into many hundreds of pages and are far too technical for continuous reading. Books for the student are seldom so interesting as to have any popular appeal.

The present book does not attempt to cater specially for either the demands of the student or the needs of the expert. For their requirements, sufficient books exist already. There is, however, a great need for a book for the ordinary reader, a book to tell the citizen, whether man or woman, what local government is all about, what is performed by means of it, and what he or she ought to expect of it.

What do those councillors do? What is it that they busy themselves with? What exactly is it that goes on inside the town hall or county hall? What is it that those officials do in those portentous municipal offices? How is it all run, and managed, and paid for? Answers to such questions as these will be found in this book.

For the man and woman who is interested, or wishes to get interested, in local government affairs, this book is intended. It cannot be exhaustive. Its size prohibits that. Its purpose is to present in outline the system and working of local government in England and Wales. Problems arising out of local government, its position in the modern state, its place in the democratic system of government, its value to the citizen, and its historical development and future trends will be discussed. No attempt will be made to give other than a broad general picture, authentic so far as its scope allows. Legal references have been reduced to a minimum, and the reader will be spared the effort of wading through the tangled undergrowth of legal provisions and decisions out of which the structure of local government has emerged.

Apart, however, from the dictates of convenience to the ordinary reader, there is a further reason why the subject of local government is, in the present book, treated without too great wealth of detail. The organization of local government administration is under review. The appointment by the Government of Local Government Commissions, one for England and one for Wales, to inquire into the organization of local government, and into the powers of local authorities, envisages the amalgamation of areas, alteration in the status of some authorities, and a redistribution of functions between neighbouring authorities. Some local authorities may go out of existence altogether. The operations of the Commissions will doubtless give a great stimulus to public interest in local affairs, and, in some localities, will give rise to not a little fuss and discussion. While all these important developments are taking place, the conscientious citizen must not be uninformed.

In the next few years many changes will probably occur in the realm of local government. There is, however, little doubt that the main structure of local government administration will remain what it is, in the hands of popularly elected county, borough, district, and parish councils, sharing functions according to status and local needs, under the general supervision of the Central Government.

It is accordingly probable that most of what is said in this book will remain current for a long time. It is hoped that the book will furnish the ordinary reader with a guide and introduction to a complex department of public administration, and will help him or her in maintaining a lively and active interest in what is, although minor and local, a none the less essential part of the organization of national democracy.

W. E. J.

April 1961

CHAPTER 1

WHAT IS LOCAL GOVERNMENT, AND WHY?

THE organization of local government in every civilized country is similar in outline. It resembles that of a large nation-wide business with local branches controlled and influenced by a central office. The degree of local independence and the measure and mode of central control vary with circumstances.

When States are small, and the administration of their affairs can be adequately attended to in all details from one central point, local government need not exist. States such as the Vatican City, Monaco, and San Marino need no local government in the modern sense. In the ancient world, when kingdoms were much smaller than in more recent times, one king with a small council could do all the work of administration both central and local. In a sense it is true to say that, in the early days of civilization, all government was local; for the areas to be governed were small. It is when nations grow big, and affairs become more complex, that the central government needs local subordinate help.

Origin and development. In earlier times, of course, government meant chiefly the maintenance of power and order. As the ruler's dominions grew, the need of local assistance to maintain his rule in the various parts of those dominions grew also. Local barons, admitting his authority, held subordinate power throughout their own lands. The story is a long one, and has many aspects. The struggle between the king and the barons resulting in this country in a curtailment

13

of royal authority and the foundation of British constitutional liberties is one important aspect which does not concern us here. But it is of interest to remember that the modern organization of local government owes some of its features to the ancient structure of local administration set up as far back as Saxon times.

As modern forms of local administration grew up, they emerged out of the old local organization. This type of development has occurred more than once in the history of English local government institutions – the old form is adapted and made to fit. This practice may be peculiarly English (we sometimes pride ourselves that it is) or it may be just a natural human tendency. Its adoption does have an effect in the maintenance of tradition and makes for a certain continuity of growth; but it also leads to many anomalies and not a little confusion and illogicality. The present shapes of the counties of England and Wales, for instance, are in very many respects quite unsuited for efficient modern administration; their shape was originally dictated by considerations which had little to do with local government as we conceive it today.

In those days, before the Norman conquest, and for very many years afterwards, there was no conception of providing local government services. Apart from such elementary matters as roads and bridges, the maintenance of public order and the suppression of crime, local services were non-existent. Poor relief, which was one of the earliest of public local services to be instituted, did not take shape until long afterwards. And of course systems of organized education and public health were quite unknown. These last-mentioned services did not become organized until towns grew to substantial size and number. In fact it is true to say that modern local government is very largely an urban affair.

Government and local government. Such early local government as existed was concerned mainly with military organization and with the suppression and punishment of crime. Present-day local government is mainly concerned with the provision of public services. Local government authorities still have concern in the organization and maintenance of the police; but in later times, particularly during the last century, there has been a gradual severance, which is by now almost complete, between the authorities responsible for providing public services and those responsible for the administration of justice. The word 'government' in association with the word 'local' has, in modern usage, a somewhat different meaning from that which it has when applied to national affairs.

The term 'government' brings to many minds the notion of interference with the activities of individuals, and their organization for national purposes. The experience of war has aided this conception. War demands much interference with the lives and work of individuals, and requires the control and direction of man power and woman power, of national resources and national morale. These functions of government have also their expression in time of peace. Such matters as the liberty of the subject, national defence, free trade and tariff reform, imports and exports, the ownership and descent of property, the relationships of husband and wife, parent and child, and master and servant are all subjects which modern national governments regard as their proper concern, and as subjects for legislation.

The business of local authorities. With these great matters local authorities have little to do. Their chief concern is with what may be called the domestic work of a civilized community. The central government will decide whether there is to be war or peace, whether agriculture or other industries

15

are to be subsidized, or taxed, or merely let alone. The rate of income tax, the imposition of estate and customs duties, the armed forces, and foreign policy, are not the affair of local authorities. What local authorities have to do is to keep the place tidy, healthy, and fit to live in, to see that the streets are swept, that the houses are properly built, to provide parks and gardens for the recreation of young and old, to educate the children, and to care for the ailing, the homeless, and the aged. This is the job of local government. It is a fine job, necessary, and one well worth doing. Without it, no civilized country can carry on, or call itself civilized.

Although in this description of the sphere of local government there is a certain insistence upon the functions of local authorities in providing public services, it must not be forgotten that local authorities (like national governments) have quite a lot to do in regulating the conduct, and to that extent interfering with the activities, of individual members of the community. An important part of the work of local government is concerned with control of this kind. The making of building by-laws to ensure that the jerry builder does not have too much of his own way; the control of petrol pumps to make sure that they are safe and not too unsightly; the licensing of cinemas and theatres and nursing homes to ensure that they are properly conducted; the sampling of food and the testing of weights and measures; the fixing of the opening hours for shops; and the making of town-planning schemes – all these involve some interference with the freedom of individuals. Failure to comply with the requirements or regulations of the local authority in respect of any of these matters is likely to involve legal proceedings and penalties. The work of local authorities touches the lives of individuals in numerous ways. The sphere of a local government authority's activities may not be on so grand a scale as that of national or international affairs; but it is very intimate and affects the citizen in all sorts of ways, from the cradle to the grave.

Modes of performing local services. This necessary work can be done in various ways. The system of local administration differs in different countries. Even in England and Wales the methods of carrying out nation-wide public services are not the same for all services. The work of the Post Office, for instance, or of the Ministry of Labour, is performed through numerous local branches, with regional groupings, and with central control. These are examples of departments of the central government, under the direct control of a member of the Cabinet – a Minister responsible to Parliament – carrying out functions in every locality through its own local officers and servants. There are other public services, organized from the centre with local branches, which are not part of the government machine but which have the status of a public authority. The National Assistance Board, the Forestry Commission, the War Damage Commission, the Milk Marketing Board are all public bodies, created by the Government, with duties to perform throughout all parts of the country. These bodies do not form part either of the machinery of the Central Government or of the local government administration properly so called.

The form in which any public service comes to be carried on seems to follow no completely settled or logical principle. In the early days of our history the difficulties of transport were among the important factors which necessitated the creation and use of local organizations. The appointment of sheriffs as representing the royal power, and of local justices of the peace, with local duties and responsibilities, and later the creation of local boards for sanitary purposes was due to the fact that in the days when these appointments were made journeys took a long time. Means of rapid communication were not available. It would have been impossible for a central department to have kept in intimate touch with operations throughout the country without some form of semi-independent local units, more or less loosely controlled. As transport and communications have improved, the possibility of organizing a national service by close control from the centre has been rendered more feasible. In cases where uniformity of administration is desired, as, for instance, in the payment of old age pensions, and the distribution of unemployment and national health insurance benefits, a closely centralized organization is nowadays possible, where it would not have been possible two hundred years ago.

Value of local government units. In the development of public services, however, during the last hundred years – a period in which the provision of public services has increased with growing speed and intensity – the form of local organization adopted for the purpose of carrying out public services has been affected by the historical fact that local organizations of great antiquity already existed throughout the country. The example provided by these local organizations has been developed; and this development has had fortunate results. It has inculcated a sense of local responsibility and local patriotism; the fact that these local organizations were to some extent democratic has had an educative effect in nurturing citizens in the practice of self-government; and, further, the growing complexity of the services which modern communities have come to regard as essential has made it more suitable to make use of semi-independent local organizations, with a certain measure of discretion and responsibility and subject to only limited supervision from the Central Government, rather than to burden the central machine with the administration of all services through its own local officers and branches.

Where the service is not required to be uniform throughout the country, where local needs differ, and where the money to be spent on the service in each locality is to come largely out of local funds, it is a useful course to make use of the local people, with intimate knowledge of local conditions, to help in the job of carrying out the service. Where there exists already the framework of a local organization, be it the county, the borough, or the parish, it is a wise practice to make use of that framework. Considerations such as these have led to the modern form of local government in this country.

The Council in local government. One of the outstanding features of local government in the United Kingdom in comparison with that of other countries is the fact that the local government organization (or at least those forms of it which have any real significance today) is invariably a council, not an individual. This was a feature of pre-Norman local organization in England; the job, such as it was, of local administration in those days was shared by more than one. Out of this feature has developed our modern jury system in which the responsibility of deciding the rights and wrongs of a dispute is shared by twelve fellow countrymen. Parliamentary government is also said to have taken its origin from this feature of early British life. The later practice, followed by successive Kings of England, of appointing local officers, earls, sheriffs, lords lieutenant, to carry the royal authority into the local areas, so that responsibility was held by individuals rather than by institutions, has faded away in this country and left these offices as survivals with but a relic of their former significance. In local government in this country today it is the council, not the official, which has the last word.

During the second world war a revival of the method of carrying central control to local levels by individual officers took place when the local Commissioners for civil defence and other similar purposes were appointed. Their appointment, although necessary and successful in times of war and emergency, was viewed with much disfavour by persons interested in local government as an impingement upon what has by now become regarded as an almost sacred principle – that local government must be the affair of a body of persons, and not of one functionary.

Foreign methods. This trend in British local government does not find a counterpart in all foreign countries. In the United States of America, although the Anglo-Saxon tradition of local councils still exists, and local county and city councils are appointed, there is a tendency to leave the greater part of the responsibility for local affairs in the hands of individuals. The Mayor of New York City, for instance, is for many practical purposes the local government authority for the City. There is a New York City Council which can make local laws and debate on municipal policy. But the Mayor himself appoints most of the principal officials and has wide administrative powers. He can even in certain circumstances veto local laws passed by the City Council. He is elected by the people. He is an instance of the survival of the notion of government by an individual rather than by a group.

Local government in France has a somewhat similar feature in that the local *maires* have a great deal of administrative power and perform duties which in the United Kingdom would be carried out by a council or a committee. Another system which has been tried in some other European countries is to appoint the heads of the various local services, education, public health, etc., in proportion to the representation of the political parties at the time of appointment, to hold paid office for a fixed term. This is a mixture of various systems and is claimed to have all the best features of all systems – democratic influence, continuity of administration, personal responsibility. The heads of the local government services form a council or have seats on the local governing body. Thus even the notion of government by a group is preserved.

In the U.S.A. and, nearer home, in the Irish Republic much use has been made of what is known as the 'city manager' system. Recognizing the fact that modern local services are, in many respects, matters for experts rather than laymen, these countries have, in some localities, accepted the idea that these services had better be left to the expert. Under the 'city manager' system the executive business of local government is not carried on by a council. A council exists, but its functions are limited, usually to general financial matters and to broad questions of policy. The work of local government as we know it is done by one man, the City or County Manager, appointed and paid by the council, given an annual budget, and a general idea of what he is to do, and then left to get on with it. He appoints his own staff. In the case of Dublin and Cork, the local councils were, for a period of years, suspended altogether by the Irish Government, and city managers appointed instead. It is alleged that the system has substantial advantages and can be adopted without loss of efficiency, indeed that it may increase efficiency. The system has its advocates in this country.

Although there may be much to be said for local government by one or several functionaries, it is doubted whether the people of this country will ever willingly part with that feature of group administration which has for many centuries been an essential part of our forms of local government.

Ancient survivals. As is only to be expected in a country where the institutions of government have developed by evolution rather than by revolution, there are still to be found many survivals of the ancient forms. Sometimes these have left a definite imprint on the present organization. In some cases the relic of ancient times is seen in established local customs; in other cases the survival is one of name only. It is in any event impossible to understand and to appreciate the modern local government system without reference to the past. British institutions have had their childhood, which, like the childhood of a living person, has influenced, and in some measure still influences, later growth.

Medieval local organization. The township – One of the earliest areas for administrative purposes was that of the township or vill. It is probably the oldest unit of minor local government and was normally a centre of population, not, of course, in the early Saxon days a very populous place, but sufficient to form a nucleus. With it were associated any outlying hamlets. The township at first had no local government organization other than what family or patriarchal influence would provide. Under Alfred the Great, however, the system of frankpledge was instituted under which all freemen in a vill were required to form themselves into groups of ten, known as tithings. Each tithing had its leader, known as tithingman or headborough. Members of each tithing were mutually responsible for one another's crimes, and, if a crime were found to have been committed by one of them, the other nine were held responsible for bringing the offender to trial. This led, of course, to a close watch

22

being kept by each member on the others and formed a primitive method of police provision.

The Manor was, broadly speaking, the medieval counterpart of a landed estate. Under the feudal system, land was parcelled out among lords, their tenants and sub-tenants, in return for military service. The manor was a unit for this purpose. The whole organization of the government of the country was bound up with land tenure. The possession of a landed estate accordingly involved official responsibilities. The lord of the manor had general supervision over the behaviour of his tenants and over any interests in and dealings in land within the manor. Manor courts existed in which tenancy questions were decided and rents were collected. This accounts for the frequent use of the term 'Court' as applied to modern country houses. These manor courts gradually extended their functions so as to include matters of a local government nature. The lord of the manor sometimes obtained from the King certain privileges, such as the inspection and control of weights and measures, and the testing of ale and bread. In such cases the manor court would deal with the matter.

When the country is organized on the basis of land tenure, the only land that can be counted for the purpose is land which is cultivated or used in some way, or, in other words, occupied land. In most cases, therefore, the area for land tenure (the manor) was coincident with the area of population (the vill or township).

The Parish was at the outset an ecclesiastical area. The most suitable places for churches were, it may be assumed, the localities where there were groups of population to form a congregation and a lord to provide patronage. Accordingly the areas for church administration tended to fall in with the areas of the manor or the township, or with groups or divisions of them. To provide money for the upkeep of the local church, the whole body of parishioners made a practice of meeting in the vestry to decide ways and means. The parishioners elected churchwardens to have the ownership of the church furniture. A rate of contribution towards church maintenance was agreed and levied by the vestry. This parish organization is the direct forerunner of the modern system of local government by elected local bodies, appointing their own officials and levying rates for local expenses.

Hundreds. The tithings were grouped into hundreds. Most of the Poor Law Unions in Norfolk and Essex in the nineteenth century corresponded in area with the hundreds into which those counties had been divided. In the counties of Sussex and Kent groups of hundreds existed, known in Sussex as *rapes* and in Kent as *lathes*. Over each hundred was appointed in Norman times a bailiff. This officer was appointed by the sheriff and was the conveyor of royal authority to the hundreds. Each hundred had a hundred court composed of the freemen of the area under the presidency of the bailiff. Hundreds in the North of England were known as *Wapentakes*, a name which still survives in some localities. The hundreds had certain duties of a local government nature to perform in the maintenance and repair of certain bridges, and it is possible that they undertook some responsibility with regard to highways. The Stewardship of the Chiltern Hundreds is still kept alive as a Crown appointment, the acceptance of which is used by Members of Parliament as a mode of resigning their seats.

The County. The hundreds were grouped in turn into counties.

In pre-Norman times each county had an earl (or count) as local governor. Here again land ownership got mixed up

24

with government. If an earl acquired a piece of land, by gift, conquest, marriage, or inheritance, he would naturally try to get it under his own governance, and have it included in his own county.

Similarly, when a church dignitary acquired lands, there was a tendency to arrange that the newly-acquired lands should be put under the same ecclesiastical jurisdiction as other lands held by the same dignitary. This doubtless also had an effect upon the parish groupings which helped to make up the area of the county.

The shapes of the ancient counties thus created have continued with little variation down to modern times. For present-day purposes the shape of these areas is not always the best for local administration. Tradition, of course, has its influence in public affairs as elsewhere. The British habit of adaptation and compromise, of making an old framework fit a new purpose, is exemplified in the persistence with which ancient areas have been accepted for changing purposes.

The Sheriff. The office of sheriff is very ancient and dates back to Saxon times. In those days the earl and the sheriff both had functions to perform in relation to the counties. In due course the powers of the earl diminished, and his rank became a title. The powers of the sheriff, however, increased as time went on. Although at the present day his office has been shorn of many of its powers, he still has very real services to perform in executing the sentences and orders of the Courts. At one period of the middle ages he was almost a minor king, but even so he had not absolute rule in each county; for each county had a court composed of all the freemen in the county. This court had some judicial work to do, but was principally a governmental assembly for the arrangement of affairs of common interest. One of the principal duties of the sheriff was to hold a sheriff's tourn twice a year by attending the hundred courts and seeing that the organization of the frankpledge was in order, and to punish offenders. The tithings were represented by the tithingmen and the vills were represented by reeves (frequently appointed by the manorial court). These representatives had to answer questions and submit reports as to any offences committed. It was from this early organization that the present jury system is said to have developed. By the fourteenth century the sheriff had become very unpopular. His appointment became annual and his duties diminished.

Justices of the Peace. As the powers of the sheriff declined, many of his duties were taken over by 'Conservators of the Peace', later known as Justices of the Peace. They were appointed by the Crown and carried out duties similar to those performed at the sheriff's tourn. Their duties grew, and by the 14th century they were exercising extensive functions of a judicial kind. They met once a quarter and, at these 'quarter sessions', with the aid of juries, tried criminal offences. They were made responsible for the supervision of vagrants, and had power to punish persons who defaulted in carrying out public duties. These powers of punishment developed into powers of an administrative kind, so that, for example, in addition to punishing a person for failure to contribute towards the repair of a highway, the justices assumed the function of directing how the highway should be maintained, and gradually, as time went on, the justices took on various non-judicial functions of a local government character.

The Constable. The office of constable was first created to ensure that the local military organization of the country was efficient. Each vill had its petty constable. Each hundred had its high constable, usually appointed at the sheriff's tourn. Their duties in relation to military organization involved the bringing of defaulters to justice. In due course the office of constable became more identified with the preservation of order and the maintenance of justice than with military affairs. As the medieval organization of the country decayed, the constables came increasingly under the control of the justices of the peace, and, in time, became, in function, akin to the constables of the present day.

Coroners were first appointed in order to keep check on the sheriff, and were accordingly persons of some consequence. They were elected by the freemen's court of the county. Their duties have shrunk considerably and now comprise the holding of inquiries (inquests) into suspicious deaths, and into the ownership of treasure trove. They are at the present day appointed by county councils, or, in some cases, by the council of a city or borough.

The Lord Lieutenant. As the sheriff's appointment became annual, he could no longer suitably carry out his military duties. It was found necessary, under the Tudor kings, to appoint a Lord Lieutenant to be responsible for organizing the armed forces in each county. He was also the chief of the county justices and was keeper of their records (custos rotulorum). His military duties now are concerned only with the organization of the auxiliary and cadet forces and are largely ceremonial.

As chief of the county justices he has an advisory committee with whose assistance he recommends to the Lord Chancellor persons for appointment as justices of the peace. He is still nominally custos rotulorum.

Ceremonially he takes precedence within the county over the sheriff, the chairman of the county council, and other office holders including (although there is some doubt about this) the mayors of cities and boroughs.

He must appoint at least twenty Deputy Lieutenants from persons who have rendered worthy service in some capacity in connexion with the armed forces.

Other ancient areas – Courts Leet. In the days when the King was the fount of all power and authority and all lesser authorities in the kingdom were deemed to hold their subordinate power by royal favour, it was a frequent practice of kings in time of war, especially during the Hundred Years War, to sell their royal rights to local lords and to other persons. As the result of this mode of raising funds, the local organizations obtained exemption from the influence and authority of the sheriff. Where a manor court obtained such a privilege, the court itself undertook the duties of the sheriff's tourn, supervised the working of the frankpledge arrangements, and appointed the petty constable for the vill, and was known, when acting for those purposes, as a 'court leet'. These courts in due course gained powers to try certain small criminal offences. There are still a number of courts leet throughout the country, but most, if not all, of them have ceased to function except for ceremonial purposes.

A *liberty* is also an area in which certain privileges inherent in the Crown have been allowed to be exercised by royal favour. The liberty of the Tower of London is an instance where this type of area has survived, if only in name. Liberties were outside the ordinary county organization. One of the ancient liberties, namely, the Isle of Ely, now forms a separate administrative county.

Soke. A soke is more or less the same thing as a liberty and is an area where special privileges are enjoyed. The Soke of Peterborough is now a separate administrative county.

Other areas of similar kind are '*honours*', of which the Honour of Pontefract is an example, being a group of

28

manors held under one lord and carrying with it certain judicial functions. A *'duchy'* and a *'county palatine'* are other instances of areas in which royal prerogatives have been delegated, particularly in regard to the holding of local courts of justice.

A *franchise* is the grant of permission to carry on a monopoly of some sort, for example, a market or a ferry.

The chartered town. One of the most important survivals of those areas where exemption from royal authority was enjoyed are the chartered towns, each of which has its own particular history, many of them going back for hundreds of years. One can imagine in those far-off days a vill or township by a river or at the confluence of two principal land routes, under the shadow of a lord's castle, busy with local trade, the prosperity of which may have been envied by the overlord. Some of these ancient towns were founded or encouraged by the overlord as an early form of estate development for the lord's benefit.

From time to time, in return for loans or gifts of money, or for other reasons, favours were obtained from the overlord or, by royal charter, from the King. These favours generally took the form of exemption from the sheriff's interference or from the authority of the overlord in certain respects. The privileges have also taken the form of licences to hold markets, privileges in relation to land tenure, or the right to own property in common as a corporation composed of the freemen of the town organized under a mayor and aldermen.

When parliamentary representation was obtained the boroughs gained the right to send their own members to Parliament. The existence of this privilege in some cases led the Crown to create deliberately a number of boroughs whose constitution did not permit the townspeople to take a share in the election. The purpose of these 'close corporations' was to obtain a return to Parliament of representatives of the boroughs who were really royal nominees.

The development of local government in the Elizabethan era. Highways. Before Queen Elizabeth I came to the throne, the system of local government, with the sheriff and the county court of freemen and the hundred and manor courts had fallen into disuse, and, although the local justices of the peace had enlarged powers, the organization was not sufficient to deal with the relief of poverty which had formerly been undertaken by the Church through the monasteries. Moreover, highways were becoming important as the prosperity of the nation grew. It accordingly became necessary to set up a new system of local administration.

The vague medieval obligation cast upon the 'inhabitants at large' to repair highways was emphasized in 1555 by an Act which made every parish responsible for the highways passing through it. The Act also provided that the constables and churchwardens were to call together the inhabitants each year to elect two surveyors of highways. These surveyors were unpaid, but forced to serve. Their duty was to name four days in each year on which the work of highway repair was to be done. The inhabitants of the parish had to supply the materials and the men. The men had to work eight hours on the job. If these services were not performed defaulters could be brought before the justices in quarter sessions, and fined. Indeed, the parish as a whole could be fined for allowing a public nuisance, i.e., a disrepaired highway, to exist. Many inhabitants as time went on preferred to pay the fine rather than take a personal share in the work. This led in due course to the modern system of collecting highway rates.

Poor Law. – Vestries. The parish organization was the

most active survival of the early English system. Each parish had its vestry and churchwardens occupied with the duty of maintaining the local church fabric. Some vestries were 'open' vestries, i.e., consisted of a meeting of all the parishioners. Other vestries were 'closed' vestries, composed of only a selected few, probably originating in a committee of an open vestry.

The parish was adopted as the unit of administration under the famous poor law of Elizabeth I, the Poor Relief Act, 1601. Each vestry had to appoint an overseer of the poor, whose function was to set the poor to useful work and to get together materials for them to work on. Poor rates were instituted in each parish on the precedent of the former church rates levied by the vestry. When, in later times, other local government duties were laid upon the vestries, the necessary money was raised by applying the procedure of the poor rate.

The Justices. The activities of the vestry and of the parish officers were supervised by the local justices of the peace. The justices had to give their sanction, for instance, to the raising of the rate and approve the appointment of a surveyor of highways. They acted as a court of appeal in the case of disputes arising out of the work of the vestry and the officers. Further, the justices had considerable power to interfere and compel the performance of the duties imposed upon the vestry. As local government services gradually became enlarged it was found advisable to give to the justices of the peace at the quarter sessions certain powers which required to be operated over a larger area. The maintenance of county bridges and the building of prisons were among the functions of quarter sessions.

The principle of local representation, which is such an essential feature of modern local government, was not very strongly expressed in the Elizabethan structure. The chartered towns existed with their local self-government and there was the vestry in each parish which could claim to represent or be formed of the local parishioners. The vestry, however, was in almost every way liable to constant interference and supervision by the justices of the peace. These justices were, of course, appointed by the Crown. They were liable to instant dismissal by the Crown and their continuity in office depended upon their ministering to the royal will. The result was that local government, although it had the form of popular representation, was very largely in the hands of the Crown.

It was the misuse of the royal power during the Stuart period, when the justices of the peace were subject to minute direction and control by the Privy Council and its committee, the Star Chamber, which led eventually during the Civil War to the breakdown of this central control over the justices of the peace, and to a corresponding increase in their local autonomy. When James II attempted to interfere with the constitution of the boroughs by trying to place them in subjection to and under scrutiny by the government, by cancelling their charters and granting new ones of his own devising, this was the last straw and was among the principal reasons which led to his being deposed.

At the revolution of 1688 it became an accepted principle that there should be no interference in local affairs by the central government. After this, the structure set up under Elizabeth I of local government through the justices of the peace continued to exist, but the justices were no longer subject to the intense supervision of the central government. The result was that local government took on that feature which is one of its principal characteristics today, namely, local self-dependence. Local government began to be local self-government. This does not mean to say that the people at large took any greater share in local affairs. The justices of the peace were still appointed by the Crown, as they are now, but being gentlemen interested in the affairs of their own counties they may be regarded as being in those days a form of local representation. In the case of boroughs which had obtained by royal charter the right to have their own set of justices or commissions of the peace, this connexion between local duties and local interests was even more intimate.

Judicial control. A measure of central control over the activities of the justices was, however, secured through the High Court. Nowadays central departments of the Government, especially the Ministries of Housing and Local Government, Education, and Transport, exercise considerable supervisory functions over the operations of local authorities. The central departments call for reports and returns, and send out inspectors to keep in touch with what local authorities are doing. Apart from all this, the local authorities are themselves responsible at law for what they do; they must keep within the ambit of their powers as laid down in Acts of Parliament; and, as owners of property and employers of labour, they have responsibilities similar to those of ordinary citizens. Accordingly, if a local authority oversteps the limits of its powers, or misuses its powers, or fails to meet its responsibilities, it can be brought before the High Court and made answerable for its defaults.

In the 18th century this judicial control by the High Court was virtually the only method by which the justices of the peace were kept under control. There was no departmental supervision as we know it today.

If the justices failed to do their duty in a particular respect, the High Court could issue a writ of Mandamus ordering the justices to do their duty; if the justices set out to do something wrong, or in excess of their duty, the High Court could issue its writ of Prohibition. A writ of Certiorari could also be issued to bring into the High Court any matter of doubt, to enable the High Court itself to determine the matter. These writs would, however, be issued only when some person sufficiently interested in or affected by the acts of the justices went to the trouble and expense of asking the High Court to issue a writ. The proceedings took the form of a lawsuit, and were applicable only to the one particular instance under dispute. The control by the High Court was therefore discontinuous, expensive, and ponderous. Hence it was in fact very little used, and, as a result, the local justices of the peace had almost undisputed and unfettered authority.

Special authorities. Local government in the 18th century was not a very live affair. The justices were often lazy or inefficient. The administration of the chartered towns (or boroughs) became corrupt, largely owing to the fact that many of them had been deliberately created merely in order to return members to Parliament, and the members of the governing bodies were kept few in number and themselves co-opted new members to fill vacancies (a 'close corporation') and were really unrepresentative of popular interests. Some large towns such as Manchester and Birmingham had no civic organization other than the local vestries and the county justices of the peace.

In the case of London the lack was very marked. The area surrounding the ancient City was developing, but the municipal area of the City was not extended to include this development. In the localities outside the City the local government was in the hands of local vestries and county justices whose functions, even if efficiently performed, were inadequate to provide, even by 18th-century standards, the local services required. Accordingly, recourse was had to the appointment of bodies of local commissioners for sewers, commissioners for paving, trustees of management of streets, and similar organizations. These were set up by special Acts of Parliament, and were semi-private concerns with powers to carry out particular duties over very limited areas. These authorities had power to levy a rate for their expenses, and most of them included, on the principle that there should be no taxation without representation, representatives elected or appointed by the local residents. The activities of these bodies within the somewhat restricted limits of the powers granted to them served to give some stimulus to local affairs.

Poor relief was in some localities handled in a somewhat similar way, by the appointment of Poor Law Corporations, with powers to build workhouses and carry out other activities for the relief of poverty. They were not a great success.

The provision of efficient main roads fell largely into the hands of turnpike trustees who were given the duty of making and maintaining what are now known as trunk roads. The old parochial organization, with its local overseers of highways, subject to the ultimate and rather distant control of local justices, was limited to areas too small to deal efficiently with national roads. The turnpike trustees, by establishing a system of main roads, of which the cost was borne by tolls levied on the road users, did a great public service, but their administration was not entirely satisfactory. The 18th century was not a period when public conscientiousness was so high as it is today. The opportunities for graft, peculation, and corruption are very limited in modern local government. In earlier times the state of affairs was very different; government was in the hands of the few, the social conscience was undeveloped; methods of business and notions of efficiency were not what they are today. There was much room for reform.

Reform of local government. It is easy to look back on the 19th century and be critical. The reformers of those days had good intentions; they had some new ideas. If they did not in fact see far enough, that is a shortcoming which perhaps every age (including the present) may in some measure be guilty of. The 19th century was a period of great reforms. A new public spirit was awakening, and a more active popular interest was being permitted in public affairs.

The reformers saw that local services must be more efficient and greater in number; they saw that some form of central control was needed. The notion of an all-purpose local authority as exemplified in the modern county borough corporation, responsible for all the local public services within the area of the borough, was not favoured. In the process of providing new services the method adopted was to create separate organizations for each service.

An epidemic of cholera in 1831 led to the creation of local temporary boards of health, with a Central Board of Health to guide and supervise them. In 1834 the poor law organization was taken in hand. Parishes were amalgamated into Unions for the purpose of granting poor relief; each Union had its elected Board of Guardians. Over all, central control was exercised by a body of Poor Law Commissioners. As the industrial revolution proceeded and towns developed, there came new needs – improved highways, street paving, and lighting, more efficient police, better public health, and, eventually, public education. For all these purposes the method in general was to set up a separate authority with powers over a special locality. The result was a most confusing pattern of authorities. There were many various types of rates, and different elections at different times for the various bodies. The areas of administration intertwined and overlapped. School boards, highway boards, sanitary authorities, burial boards, poor law unions all existed together, side by side with the vestries, boroughs, and the justices of the peace, who still retained some of the administrative functions. To modern eyes the picture of local government in the middle of the 19th century is an administrative nightmare, a tangle of authorities, unrelated to one another either in area or function, and with little coherence or uniform direction from above. The newly created local authorities, however, had in general the feature of popular election.

Towards the end of the century the structure of local government was considerably simplified. In 1871 the Local Government Board was created, as the central department of State with general supervision over local government matters. Under the Public Health Act, 1872, the country was mapped out into urban and rural sanitary areas. By the Municipal Corporations Act, 1882, the organization of the boroughs was reformed, and their powers and duties were readjusted. The Local Government Act, 1888, created county boroughs from the larger towns, and administrative counties from the ancient counties, and set up popularly elected councils for each of these areas. In 1894, urban and rural district councils were created outside London from the former sanitary authorities, and parish organization was modernized. In 1899 London local government was reformed by the creation of the metropolitan borough councils.

In 1902 the organization of public education was simplified by the abolition of the former school boards, and the transfer of public education responsibilities to the county councils and other local government authorities. This is an example

37

of the movement which took place in favour of the emergence of the local government authorities – county councils, borough councils, urban and rural district councils – as composite authorities, having general functions. A further great example was provided by the Local Government Act, 1929, which transferred poor law functions to the county councils and county borough councils, and abolished the poor law Guardians. In 1919 the Local Government Board was abolished and the Ministry of Health was set up with general duties of supervision over all local government authorities. This general duty was, in 1951, transferred to the newly-created Ministry of Housing and Local Government. The Ministry of Health remained responsible for the National Health Service.

The Local Government Act, 1933, codified the constitution and general powers of the six types of local government authority which now exist outside London – County Councils, County Borough Councils, Non-County Borough Councils, Urban District Councils, Rural District Councils, and Parish Councils. Although the various powers and duties of these different types of local authority are complex, the law relating to the internal structure of the authorities, the mode of their election, their membership, their officials, and their general financial arrangements has been clarified and simplified. The London Government Act, 1939, carried out a similar codification and clarification in respect of the London County Council and the Metropolitan Borough Councils.

CHAPTER 2

WHO ARE THE LOCAL AUTHORITIES?

THE citizen who sets out to understand what local government is and how it operates is likely to be confused at first at the number of local bodies exercising functions in his locality. He sees on the municipal vehicles, on the notices at the entrances to the local park, and on the periodical demands for rates which he receives, the name of a local council. But at the same time he realizes that not all the public services in his locality are run by a council. He sees references in the local press to county courts, to borough magistrates or justices, and he may have received himself the thanks of the county for serving on a jury. And he may have noticed the curious fact that whereas the public houses on one side of the street close at 10 p.m., the public houses on the other side of the street close at 10.30 – which leads him to suppose that the control of licensed premises is also a matter of local administration.

Local government authorities properly so called have one feature in common, which serves to distinguish them from the other instruments of local administration. Local government authorities are, all of them, popularly elected by persons resident or carrying on business in the area over which the local government authority operates.

To help towards a clearer understanding of what local government authorities are, it may be convenient to dispose briefly of certain types of local body which, although exercising local functions, do not possess the essential feature of popular election.

Public Utility Corporations. Certain public utility services, namely the supply of water, the provision of omnibuses, the maintenance of public markets, and the management of ports and harbours, are sometimes carried on by private enterprise in some form, often by means of companies having, like other companies carrying on commercial undertakings, a body of shareholders and a board of directors. These are, of course, not local authorities, although they have some authority and their activities are local, and although the services they provide are essential and the companies are, to some extent, under an obligation to the public and may be to some extent controlled or limited in their activities accordingly.

These services may, however, be carried on by the local council, in which case the council will be both local government authority and public utility supplier. In some cases the public utility service may be entrusted to a Board, specially constituted under Act of Parliament. These boards are public in that their operations are carried on not for private profit but for the public benefit, and they are responsible to or subject to supervision by some Government Department. There may even be, on the board, representatives of the local government authorities for the areas in which the board's undertaking is carried on. The board may perhaps, like the Metropolitan Water Board, have power to levy a water rate based on rateable value of occupied property, and irrespective of the amount of water consumed by the payer. They may have powers to interfere with private property, by the laying of mains or overhead wires. They may even have powers to run a private police force to protect their property. But all these Boards, Corporations, Companies, and other public bodies are not local government authorities; for they all lack the essential element of popular election by local constituents.

Local administration of justice. The whole of England and Wales is divided into areas for the administration of justice. The general basis of this division is the area of the ancient counties and boroughs. Commissions of the Peace have been issued to local justices of the peace, who have power to hold petty sessional courts where minor offences may be tried, and to hold quarter sessions, that is courts meeting at least once a quarter, at which all the local justices may attend, and at which more serious offences may be tried. The most serious offences of all are tried only at assizes held by a High Court judge in each county periodically. At the same time, for civil disputes, not involving a crime, there are the County Courts, each presided over by a paid and properly qualified County Court judge, while the more important civil disputes can be tried at assizes by the High Court judge and certain very small non-criminal matters may be dealt with by the local justices of the peace. The expense of providing and carrying on the County Courts (for civil disputes) is borne by the Central Government.

This terse reference to the system of administering justice locally is intended merely to emphasize that local government authorities are not concerned with the holding of courts and the trial of offences or disputes. They are, however, concerned in one unobtrusive yet important feature: they have to contribute towards the expenses of the administration of justice, at assizes, quarter sessions, and petty sessions. The extent of their concern in this respect will be dealt with later. One thing should be borne in mind – that the areas for the administration of justice are not always coincident with the areas for local government administration.

Liquor Licensing. For the sale of intoxicants, by retail,

two licences are required, one issued by the Board of Customs and Excise, and one by the local justices of the peace. The justices' licence must be obtained before an excise licence can be granted. For the purpose of issuing justices' licences the country is divided into licensing districts. In each district there is a committee of 'licensing justices' who act as a court for the granting and renewal of liquor licences. When a new licence has been granted the licence must be confirmed. The authority for confirming the licence is, in a county, a committee of quarter sessions, or, in a borough, a committee of the borough justices. There are similar committees which act as the local compensation authority for assessing and granting compensation for licences extinguished.

Local licensing justices have various powers of control over licensed premises, such as the fixing of the hours of opening and approval of the structural arrangements of the premises. The justices are also concerned with the registration and control of clubs where intoxicants are sold. The local organization for licensing the sale of intoxicants is clearly distinguishable from the organization of local government authorities. In some localities the licensing justices issue, as well as liquor licences, licences to authorize the use of premises for public music and dancing.

Local government authorities. The organization of local government authorities varies in different parts of the country. Generally speaking, in large towns outside London, there is only one local government authority. In other parts of the country there may be two or three authorities exercising local government functions in the same area.

It is always useful when discussing a subject, especially a somewhat complex subject like local government, to get the terminology clearly understood – to know the proper meaning of the words involved. In local government matters a number of terms frequently crop up, such as Borough, City, Corporation, County. It may be well to consider before going further what it is that these terms signify.

A *Borough* is a town with a certain legal status. A 'parliamentary borough' is a town which forms in itself a parliamentary constituency and elects its own member or members of parliament. The term has no local government significance.

In the local government sense a borough is a town with a corporate status. The borough is a corporate body or legal 'person' with rights, powers, and property. The corporate body may consist of the Mayor, Aldermen, and Burgesses, or, if the borough is a City, the Mayor, Aldermen, and Citizens. The burgesses were in olden times the freemen of the borough, consisting of those traders, residents, and property owners in the borough who enjoyed the right of voting at borough elections. The burgesses or freemen had also a share in the corporate property. In modern times burgesses or freemen are ratepayers and, as electors and ratepayers, are for local government purposes in the same position as other electors and ratepayers.

Freedom of a borough. In boroughs where the corporate body owns private property, the rank of burgess or freeman brings with it certain rights to share in that property. It is for that reason that various advantages such as educational scholarships, charities, the admission to or nomination to local almshouses can be enjoyed only by burgesses or persons having the status of the freedom of the borough. This status can be acquired in various ways, by residence, by marriage or near kinship with a freeman, or by being bound an apprentice to a freeman. But you cannot become a freeman of a borough by buying the right or by having it given to you. The City of London, however, being an exception to this rule, makes a practice of conferring its full freedom by gift upon distinguished persons. In boroughs generally the council of the borough may confer, as a gift, the honorary freedom of the borough upon anyone it likes; but this honorary freedom confers no right to share in borough property.

The Borough Council. The corporate body therefore consists of all the residents and other freemen or burgesses. All the functions of the corporate body are, however, exercisable by the Council, consisting of the Mayor, Aldermen, and Councillors.

In the case of metropolitan boroughs, modern creations brought into existence in 1899, there are no burgesses or freemen, although honorary freedom may be conferred. The corporate body in the case of these boroughs consists of the Mayor, Aldermen, and Councillors.

Outside London boroughs are of two kinds, County Boroughs and non-county Boroughs. These will be discussed later on.

The term *City* is a title of honour conferred by the Crown upon a town. Sometimes the mayor is also given the title of Lord Mayor. These titles have ceremonial significance only. Other titles are sometimes conferred as marks of honour without any local government significance. Hence the Metropolitan Borough of Kensington is, by virtue of Letters Patent, called the Royal Borough of Kensington, although it has exactly the same legal powers and status as other Metropolitan Boroughs. The title 'Regis' as in Bognor Regis, Lyme Regis, and the word 'Royal' in Royal Tunbridge Wells are other instances of marks of royal favour.

A Corporation means, in law, a body or society authorized by law to act as an individual. From what has been said above it will be seen that boroughs are all corporations.

The term 'Municipal Corporation' is applied to them all. In many boroughs the use of the term corporation is preferred by the local people. The official letter paper will in the case of some of the boroughs bear the heading 'Borough of Blank'. In other cases it will be 'Blank Corporation'. Most of them seem to prefer the latter, thinking it more impressive. The term corporation is, in strict law, applicable to all sorts of bodies, limited liability companies, learned societies, and county councils, for instance, but in local government usage the term is applied only to boroughs, or cities. When the borough has, however, been created a city, preference is given to the higher title. In such a case the letter heading would be 'City of Blank' or, rather more formal and correct, 'Corporation of the City of Blank'.

Even in the local government world, among the impersonal entities of corporations, there can, as in the social world of living persons, be quite a lot of sensitiveness about the correct use of names and titles.

The term '*county*' is a little difficult to explain; for it has a twofold significance. It means a certain area for judicial purposes, and a different area for local government purposes. Most maps of England and Wales show, in varied colours, 53 counties. Some show 52, the map-maker being under the erroneous impression that there is no County of London (which there is). These counties, descended from their medieval counterparts, are, broadly speaking, the areas used for the administration of justice. But, since medieval times, the rise of boroughs and towns has resulted in the cutting away of certain town areas from the area of the counties. Some boroughs obtained, by royal charter, the right to establish their own courts of quarter sessions presided over by a special magistrate known as a Recorder. Some boroughs have a separate commission of the Peace that is, a set of Justices of the Peace for the borough separate from the county justices. Some boroughs have the proud title of a 'County of a City' or a 'County of a Town'. These may have their own separate sheriffs, coroners, and assize courts and could be entirely independent of the county for judicial purposes.

To the extent to which a borough has its own local judicial system, which it pays for itself, it does not need to avail itself of the system of county justice. Borough courts have, however, limited powers, and can try only a certain range of offences. Accordingly, in boroughs which have not the full status of a county, there are still some matters for which the borough may have to make use of the county system. The extent of this use varies according to local conditions. It will be seen, then, that a borough may be within a county for some judicial purposes, and outside a county for other judicial purposes, or, indeed, outside it altogether.

In so far as a borough makes use of the system of county justice a contribution (varying according to the use which is made) has to be paid towards the county expenses. These county expenses are met eventually out of the county rates made by the county council. Because the county council acts as paymaster for the expenses of administering justice, such as the building and repair of court houses, the salaries of clerks to the courts and other staff, there is in each county a Standing Joint Committee composed of representatives of the justices and of the county council, to deal with all such matters. This Standing Joint Committee is also the authority for maintaining the county police force.

For local government purposes there have been created what are known as 'administrative counties'. Of these, there are 62 in England and Wales, including London. Their areas do not always coincide with the area of judicial counties; for in some cases more than one administrative county has been formed from the area of one judicial county, and besides this, the county boroughs are independent of the administrative counties and form no part of them.

It will be appreciated, therefore, that if the maps of England and Wales showing the counties were strictly accurate, there would be, in most of the counties, blank spots representing those cities, boroughs, and towns which, for one purpose or another, are not in any county at all.

For ordinary day-to-day purposes, and to avoid making an elaborate explanation every time the term 'county' is used, the term 'geographical county' has been devised. It serves to indicate the area of an ancient county together with the boroughs and judicial counties of cities and towns which, although outside the county in some senses, are geographically embedded in it or adjacent to it, and are generally allied with it. It is not entirely a satisfactory term; for counties for the most part are merely artificial areas devised for governmental purposes, and bear little relationship to physical geography, except where, as in the case of the County of Anglesey, which is an island, the area of the county is delimited by geographical conditions.

Local government authorities outside London. The pattern of local government organization laid down by the Local Government Act, 1933, is simple, in that it provides for only six types of local government units outside London – administrative counties, county boroughs, non-county boroughs, urban districts, rural districts, and parishes. For the purpose of map-drawing the pattern on the whole is uncomplicated. The country is first divided up into two sorts of areas – administrative counties and county boroughs. For each of these there is a council to administer local government services within the area. The county boroughs are self-contained units for local government purposes, and no other local government authority exercises powers within the area of a borough of this class.

The administrative counties, other than London, are subdivided into county districts. These county districts may be either a non-county borough, an urban district, or a rural district. Each has its own council. Each of these county districts is divisible into parishes; but in the areas of boroughs and urban districts parishes have for the most part little, if any, local government significance. In the rural districts, however, parishes have their own local organizations by way of parish council or parish meeting which take a small but quite definite part in local administration.

It will be seen then that since the administrative counties are divided up into smaller areas which each have councils, there will be in respect of any part of an administrative county at least two local authorities, the county council and the council of the county district. In the rural parts of an administrative council there will be the parish organization as well.

While therefore the basic structure of local government organization may be simple enough, the administration has certain complexities due to the interrelation of the various local authorities.

County Boroughs. Leaving aside London, which has a peculiar local government structure of its own, which will be dealt with later, let us consider the easiest case first. In the First Schedule to the Local Government Act, 1933, will be found a list of 83 towns in England and Wales which have the status of County Boroughs. This status was first given to towns by the Local Government Act, 1888. The towns which were by that Act created county boroughs were either Counties of a city or of a town or had a population of not less than 50,000. Of the original number created one or two have disappeared by merger into adjoining areas. A number of new ones have been created since 1888. All of the towns enjoying this status are considered to be large enough to be able to run all their own local government services – education, public health, police, housing, and town planning, etc. They are all-purpose local authorities, levying their own rates, spending their own money and responsible to and supervised by no other local authority. The area of the borough is, for election purposes, divided into wards.

Creation and extension of county boroughs. New county boroughs can come into existence, and the area of existing ones be extended, only by the authority of the Central Government. Formerly the Minister of Health, at the instance of the local authority seeking this status or an extension, made, after due inquiry, a provisional Order which, when confirmed by Parliament, had the effect of an Act of Parliament. The local authority could, alternatively, itself promote in Parliament a special Act. From 1926, borough status could be acquired only by promoting a special Act and only if the population of the area concerned was 75,000 or upward. Nowadays a population of at least 100,000 is usually necessary.

The Minister of Housing and Local Government now has the function of submitting to Parliament Orders for the creation or extension of county boroughs; this will usually be done on the recommendation of the appropriate Local Government Commission. Until 1973 a local authority may not itself promote in Parliament a Bill for these purposes. The functions of the Commissions are dealt with more particularly in Chapter 9.

Administrative counties outside London. The first schedule to the Local Government Act, 1933, gives a list of 61 administrative counties in England and Wales (excluding London). These units were first created in 1888 and were based primarily on the areas of the ancient counties. Some of these counties were already sub-divided into parts, with separate Commissions of the Peace. Accordingly in certain special instances the area of the ancient county was used to form two or more administrative counties. Of those in the list given in the Act of 1933, the majority will be familiar in name to everyone. It will be noticed, however, that each of the three Ridings of Yorkshire is a separate administrative county. East Suffolk and West Suffolk, and East Sussex and West Sussex, the three parts of Lincolnshire (Holland, Kesteven, and Lindsey) are each separate administrative counties. The ancient county of Cambridge is two – the Isle of Ely being one, and the rest of Cambridge the other. Similarly the northern portion of Northamptonshire forms the Administrative County of the Soke of Peterborough (the smallest one of all), and the rest of the county is the Administrative County of Northampton. Since 1889 the Isle of Wight has been made a separate administrative county and the remainder of Hampshire forms the Administrative County of Southampton.

New administrative counties can be created, and their boundaries altered, by authority of the Central Government, in the same way as the creation and extension of county boroughs.

Each administrative county has a popularly elected County Council, which consists of a chairman, county aldermen, and county councillors, and is a body corporate, with a common seal.

The area of an administrative county is sub-divided for election purposes into electoral divisions, each of which returns one councillor. For administrative purposes the area is divided into county districts and parishes. The county districts are either non-county boroughs, urban districts, or rural districts. The county council shares with the councils of the county districts the work of local government, and has certain powers of supervision over them.

Non-County Boroughs are, in organization, very similar to County Boroughs. They have each an elected council composed of a Mayor, Aldermen, and Councillors. The Mayor, Aldermen, and Burgesses (or, in the case of a borough which is a city, the Mayor, Aldermen, and Citizens) form a body corporate.

Most of the boroughs are towns of great antiquity. They came into existence at various times by virtue of Royal Charters or special Acts of Parliament. The list of them given in the Local Government Act, 1933, numbers 273. New boroughs of this class are formed by Royal Charter applied for by the council of an urban or rural district desiring to obtain borough status. The Charter will contain details of the number of borough councillors, the wards for electoral purposes, and the number of councillors for each ward.

The powers and duties of the Council of a non-county Borough are, for the most part, comparable with those of an Urban District Council. If local conditions warrant it, the Crown may grant to a new borough a separate Commission of the Peace.

The boundary of a non-county borough can be altered in the same way as that of a county borough.

The grant of a charter from the Crown has a special effect upon the legal position of the borough corporation. A chartered corporation has all the powers of an ordinary person and may do any lawful act which is not expressly forbidden by its charter. Other authorities, such as urban district councils, may do only what Parliament has expressly given them power to do. Boroughs are therefore considered to be in the superior position.

Besides all this there is, of course, a great stimulus to local patriotism and civic pride in obtaining the status of a borough, with a mayor and aldermen in all their regalia, a town clerk with a wig, and the other ceremonial features.

Urban Districts and Rural Districts are descendants of the old urban and rural sanitary districts of a county, and the urban districts are, in practice, the built-up areas, and the rural districts are the less populated parts. The council of an urban or of a rural district consists of a chairman and councillors only, and is a body corporate with a common seal. The local government powers of an urban district council are somewhat less than those of a non-county borough, and rather more than those of a rural district council.

Proposals for the alteration of the areas or status of urban and rural districts may be made in certain cases by the county council and in other cases by the appropriate Local Government Commission. For further particulars see Chapter 9.

County councils have powers to deal with the division of urban and rural districts into wards for electoral purposes and to settle or alter the number of councillors for each ward. Urban district councils may also put forward their own proposals. Copies of orders made by a county council under these powers must be sent for information to the Home Secretary and Minister of Housing and Local Government.

The Parish. There are over 11,000 parishes in England and Wales. These have developed out of the old ecclesiastical parishes but are nowadays not always identical with them. In rural districts the parishes are primary units for rating and local government purposes. In urban areas parishes are of no local government importance, since the rating areas in urban districts and boroughs are now identical with the urban district or borough. In urban areas the parish has no separate local government organization. There is no need for it in towns; for the area administered by the town councils is compact and relatively closely knit.

In the sparsely populated countryside, however, the civic consciousness of the inhabitant arises around a local village or hamlet. It is a long way to the county town, the seat of county administration, and the relations between village and county council are likely to be less intimate than between the burgess and his borough council. Even the existence of a rural district council does not bring local administration in the countryside to the same level of relationship between the elector and the elected governing body as is, or could be, the case in town areas.

In the thinly populated rural districts there was accordingly considered to be greater need for the establishment of smaller local units, not only to give the villagers an opportunity for expression of local public opinion, but also to aid the rural district council in the administration of their relatively large and scattered areas.

Accordingly, in every parish a 'parish meeting' of all the local government electors must be called together in March each year. In parishes with a population of 300 or more a parish council also must be elected. In parishes of less population parish councils may be appointed by order of the county council. The county council has power to divide parishes into wards for parish council elections and may also amalgamate parishes under one parish council. If there is no parish council the parish meeting must meet at least twice a year. Parish areas may be altered by order of the Minister of Housing and Local Government after consideration by either the county council or the appropriate Local Government Commission.

The functions of the parish are, of course, minor. They relate to such matters as footpaths, public clocks, public lighting, parking places, village greens, allotments, and the suppression of nuisances. A parish council has slightly larger powers than a parish meeting.

In some cases the acts of a parish council must be confirmed by the parish meeting. Similarly, decisions of a parish meeting must, if there is sufficient demand made at the meeting, be confirmed by a referendum of all the electors in the parish. A parish council is a body corporate. If there is no parish council, the parish property is vested in a 'representative body' consisting of the chairman of the parish meeting and the members representing the parish on the rural district council. Neither the parish council nor the representative body has a common seal. The acts of these bodies can be legally signified only by the signatures and personal seals of selected members.

London. The local government arrangements in London differ somewhat from those of other parts of the country. This difference is due to some extent to historical causes and to some extent to the special conditions existing in London by virtue of its size and importance as the national capital.

During the early part of the 19th century the organization of local government here had much the same features as elsewhere. There was the ancient City of London, with its corporate status, with Lord Mayor, Aldermen, and Councillors, and the rank of a city and of a county, with separate sheriffs and quarter sessions. Around the old city were the ancient counties of Middlesex, Kent, Surrey, and Essex, governed by justices of the peace and vestries. The increasing urban development led to the appointment of numerous trusts and boards of commissioners with powers relating to the paving of streets, sewerage, etc., over very limited areas. By 1855 there were some 300 of these bodies operating in the area which came to be known as the 'Metropolis'. By the Metropolis Management Act of 1855, these local bodies were abolished and provision was made for their powers to be carried out by administrative vestries for the larger parishes, and district boards for groups of the smaller parishes. Over all this, a Metropolitan Board of Works was set up which was elected, not directly by the people, but by the City Corporation, the administrative vestries and the district boards. In 1888, when administrative counties were created, an Administrative County of London was formed out of the area of the Metropolis and, at the same time, a 'County of London' was formed for judicial purposes, with separate sheriff and quarter sessions. The City remained a separate judicial county, but forms part of the Administrative County. In 1899, the administrative vestries and district boards were supplanted by twenty-eight Metropolitan Borough Councils. One of these, Westminster, has the title of City, but this is a difference only of name.

There are no county boroughs within the geographical area of the Administrative County of London; neither are there any county districts or any local government parishes.

The work of local government in the Administrative County is shared between the London County Council, the City Corporation, and the Metropolitan Borough Councils. The City Corporation, although it has a unique position as regards powers and duties, is not an all-purpose authority like the council of a county borough. The Metropolitan Borough Councils are in a position somewhat comparable with that of a non-county borough. They are bodies corporate, with Mayors, Aldermen, and Councillors. In the areas of the City and of the Metropolitan Boroughs, the London County Council has functions. (As to these, see Chapter 4.)

The boundaries of the Administrative County of London, of the City of London, and of the Metropolitan Boroughs can be altered only by Act of Parliament. For the purpose of parliamentary and county council elections there are forty-three constituencies in the Administrative County. The boundaries of these areas do not correspond with, and in some cases cut across, those of the cities and boroughs. The City and boroughs are sub-divided into wards for the election of city and borough councillors.

Special bodies having functions in London. The special needs of London have led to the creation of special authorities for police, passenger transport, and water supply and certain other purposes. Mention is made of these here not only to complete the picture of London local government but also because the special bodies which have been set up provide examples of the various types of local body to which, either as an experiment or to meet the needs of a particular case, duties ordinarily entrusted to local government authorities can be given.

The City Corporation has its own police force operating in the area of the city. In the surrounding area covering a belt of from twelve to fifteen miles radius from Charing Cross and known as the Metropolitan Police Area, police powers are exercised by a Commissioner of Police for the Metropolis and five Assistant Commissioners. These are appointed by the Crown and are under the direct supervision of the Home Secretary. The ordinary local government authorities in the Metropolitan Police Area have no police functions. All the local authorities have to do is to pay out of the rates their due share of the expenses of the Force.

Passenger transport, including motor omnibuses, trolley-buses, tramcars, tube railways, and (if need be) Thames steamboats are, in and around London, a monopoly of the London Transport Executive, which is not elected at all but is appointed by the Minister of Transport, and acts as the agent of the British Transport Commission. The area in which the Executive can operate extends far outside the boundary of the Administrative County.

Water supply is provided, both in London and for a considerable distance outside London, by the Metropolitan Water Board, which is an indirectly elected body of eighty-eight members. These members are elected by the London County Council, the City Corporation, the Metropolitan Borough Councils, and other local authorities in the area of the Board's operations. The Board raises its funds by the levy of a direct water rate upon occupiers of property.

The conservancy and management of the River Thames from the sea to Teddington (Middlesex), and of the Port of London are entrusted to the Port of London Authority, which is partly elected by wharfingers, watermen, and other users of the port, and partly appointed by the Admiralty, the Minister of Transport, Trinity House, the London County Council, and the City Corporation.

Above Teddington, the river is administered by the Thames Conservancy, a body consisting of nominees of government departments and local authorities.

To the man in the street 'London' means the vast urban agglomeration near the mouth of the Thames. In the popular sense the word is not confined to administrative boundaries. The urban development has overflowed far beyond the ancient city and well beyond the County of London. Outside the County the ordinary framework of local government is in existence. Counties, county boroughs, non-county boroughs, and urban districts all border on the county boundary and, in the social and economic senses, form part of the national capital and share with it and each other many problems.

The existence of so many authorities, all carrying out different duties in and around London, themselves each having a different sphere of operations, presents a rather complex pattern to the citizen and involves special problems for those engaged in the local government administration.

Joint authorities. Some of the examples given above indicate that some local bodies are formed of nominees appointed by existing local authorities. There are many local bodies of this sort up and down the country. The commonest form is that of a joint board or joint committee. Local authorities with common problems or common interests have, for various purposes, power to get together by nominating representatives to a joint board or by appointing a joint committee to carry out some particular service over the area of the local authorities concerned. Joint boards may be appointed for sewerage purposes, for providing water supply, local health services, cemeteries, and other purposes. These joint boards are generally created by Act of Parliament or by ministerial order having the force of law. They frequently have corporate status, although their funds are mostly provided by compulsory contributions from the appointing authorities.

Joint committees are appointed by local authorities for such purposes as town planning, education, and the provision of public open spaces. Their existence depends upon the continuous support of the various appointing authorities. In some cases the acts of a joint committee need the ratification of the appointing bodies; and in most cases an appointing authority, by withdrawing its financial support or refusing to appoint representatives, can bring a joint committee's operations to an end. On the other hand, the device of appointing joint committees enables the administration of local services to overflow beyond the boundary of one local authority and to be carried on in composite areas according to the requirements of operational efficiency. The possible combinations of local authorities for these purposes are very varied. As a means of imparting flexibility to local government organization, joint committees are much favoured in some quarters. Too great use of them tends towards the dangers of over-complication and incoherence – the wood gets too full of trees. The more local bodies there are, the more difficult is the task of the administrator who has to manage, reconcile, and satisfy them all.

In this, as in all the other branches of local government, however, goodwill and the desire to cooperate for the public benefit can overcome many difficulties, whereas, if the will is lacking, the most perfectly designed organization will never produce efficient results.

CHAPTER 3

THE CONSTITUTION AND ELECTION OF LOCAL GOVERNMENT AUTHORITIES

THE principle of democratic representation is an essential feature of all the types of local government authority – county councils, borough councils, district councils, and parish councils. None the less it is oddly enough quite possible for a person to become an influential member of any of these bodies without having had to submit himself to popular election. The reason is that each of these various types of council has itself a certain limited power to make an election. In the case of county councils, urban and rural district councils, and parish councils, the chairman of the council need not be a member of the council at the time of his election as chairman. He must, however, be qualified to be a member – that is, he must have the same qualifications as a candidate for popular election as a councillor needs to have. As soon as the council elects him chairman he becomes a full member of the council.

In the case of county, non-county, and metropolitan boroughs, the presiding member of the council is the mayor (or Lord Mayor in large cities). Here again, it is not necessary to be already a member of the borough council in order to get elected as Mayor. The Mayor may be appointed either from among the members of the council or from among the ordinary members of the public, so long as he has the qualifications which a candidate has to have to get elected as councillor.

Aldermen. County councils, and borough councils

whether county, non-county, or metropolitan, have another set of appointments within their power. Each of these councils has a group of members known as aldermen. These aldermen have to have the same electoral qualifications as councillors, but they are not elected by the public; they are elected by the council itself. These aldermen, in the case of counties and boroughs outside London, form one quarter of the membership of the council. In other words, they are equal in number to one-third of the number of councillors. In the case of London County Council and the Metropolitan Borough Councils, the aldermen are equal in number to one-sixth of the number of councillors. In other words, one-seventh of the council is made up of aldermen.

Use of appointments from outside the council. It is therefore possible to become a mayor, chairman, or alderman without being elected by the people at large. This possibility is often made use of by local authorities. A chairman or a mayor has generally a great number of ceremonial duties to perform, besides being a member of the council. These duties involve much time, and not a little personal expense. There are accordingly occasions when a council has some difficulty in finding a person free to act both as member of the council and as its ceremonial representative. It is therefore an advantage to be able to offer this dignity to some worthy (and duly qualified) local citizen free of the hurly-burly of popular election.

In the same way, the appointment of aldermen is of use in providing an additional opportunity of bringing into the service of the public persons with suitable temperament and experience who do not desire to get too greatly mixed up in local politics. Use is sometimes made of the appointment of aldermen to secure the continued service of members of long standing who have not managed to secure re-election as councillors. Where the local council is influenced by political feeling the party in the majority on a council can, by appointing its own supporters to fill vacancies among the aldermen, strengthen its majority. There is generally between the parties a gentlemen's agreement to appoint the aldermen so that the party representation among them is similar in proportion to that of the councillors.

Aldermen can be elected from among the existing councillors; but the general tendency is to make the appointments from among persons who are not already members of the council. This is because a person cannot be both councillor and alderman. If a councillor is made an alderman he ceases to be a councillor; a vacancy is created among the councillors, and a by-election must be held.

The Chairman or Mayor remains in office for one year only. He is, during that year, by virtue of his office, a local justice of the peace. If he was already at his appointment a member of the council, his appointment as chairman or mayor does not cause a vacancy among the ordinary members; the chairman or mayor still remains a member. On the other hand, if the chairman or mayor is elected from outside the existing members of the council, no one on the council has to move out to make room for him. His appointment in fact adds (in such a case) one more member to the council.

Salary of a Chairman or Mayor. Any type of council, other than a parish council, may pay to the chairman or mayor such remuneration as the council thinks fit. Many local authorities refrain from making use of this power. There is still a strong feeling that the service given to the public by members of local authorities ought to be unpaid, and that the payment of salaries to members may lead to abuses, place-mongering, and the machinations of careerists.

On this much can, no doubt, be said. The fact remains that a chairman of a council, and still more, a mayor, has a ceremonial position. The mayor has precedence (subject to the royal prerogative) over every one else in the borough. People expect these functionaries to act up to their position, to lay foundation stones, preside at meetings, and attend on distinguished visitors, all of which brings with it expense either in dispensing hospitality or in obtaining formal clothes or personal transport. Many suitable men and women with a good record of public service behind them will hesitate to accept the office of mayor, or of chairman, because of the expense involved. Some local authorities compromise, and pay the expense of a car for the use of their presiding member. Some bodies, like the London County Council, pay no salary to their chairman, but provide a ceremonial fund. The Corporation of the City of London gives the Lord Mayor a salary of £15,000 a year. Some other Cities pay a mayoral salary but very much less in amount.

Such a salary paid to the chairman or mayor should not really be regarded as a salary in the sense of being an income for the job. It should properly be regarded as a compensation for the expense involved in carrying out the duties and ceremonial obligations of the office and in providing official hospitality which would otherwise have to be paid for out of the chairman's (or mayor's) own pocket.

Deputy Mayor. In Boroughs outside London the mayor appoints his own deputy, if one is required. The deputy mayor does not become by virtue of his office a justice of the peace. He may not preside over any meeting of the borough council unless the meeting has specially authorized him to do so. In other respects he may discharge, in the absence of the mayor, all the mayor's functions. A deputy mayor must be a member of the council before he can be appointed; he cannot be paid by the council. He holds office for a year.

In the case of metropolitan boroughs the deputy mayor is appointed by the council itself from among its own members. He can act as chairman of the council in the absence of the mayor without further authorization. He does not become a justice of the peace by virtue of his office. The council cannot pay him.

Vice-chairman. County councils must appoint a vice-chairman. Every other council may appoint one if it wishes. The vice-chairman is appointed from among the existing members. He cannot be paid, and does not become a justice of the peace by virtue of his office. He holds office for a year. The London County Council, in addition to appointing an unpaid vice-chairman, has also power to appoint a deputy chairman who may be paid, but, although the Council appoints each year a deputy chairman, he in practice receives no salary.

Term of office of members. From what has been said, it will have been appreciated that the body of the members of a local council may consist either of aldermen and councillors (county councils and boroughs), or of councillors alone.

A chairman, mayor, vice-chairman, and deputy mayor must each be appointed annually. Councillors, however, whether of parish councils, borough councils, or county councils, serve for three years. Aldermen serve for six years.

Retirement in Counties and London Boroughs. In the case of a county council or a metropolitan borough council, the working of this arrangement is quite simple. At the end of every three years the whole body of councillors goes out of office and a general election of councillors is held. But only half the aldermen go out of office – that half which has been in office the longer. Accordingly when the new council is elected, it finds half the former aldermen still in office, and it has to fill up the vacancies by appointing the other half.

Retirement in Boroughs outside London. In the case of boroughs outside London the situation is rather complicated; for it is not the rule with them to have a general election of councillors every three years. Although each councillor as an individual holds office for three years, the whole body of the councillors do not stop in office for three years. One third of the councillors go out of office each year. This means that in a borough outside London there is a local election every year – for one-third of the councillors.

The aldermen, however, hold office for six years. Half of them retire (as in the case of county aldermen) every third year. For two years there is no election of aldermen; but in every third year there is an election of half of them.

This periodical retirement of councillors and aldermen does not prevent the re-election of the same individuals as and when the time for their retirement comes round.

The idea of all this partial periodical retirement is to make for continuity in administration. At any point of time in a borough council's career, there is always a remnant of a former council among the members. There can never be, in such a borough, such a complete landslide among the membership as happens sometimes at parliamentary elections when a complete change-over of national political feeling takes place.

Retirement in urban and rural district and parish councils. In the case of parish councils, the whole of the members retire every third year. Similarly in the case of a number of urban and rural district councils, the whole body of councillors retire together at the end of their third year. There are no aldermen, and the position is therefore uncomplicated.

But, so far as urban and rural district councils are concerned, this simplicity can be achieved only in special cases. The normal procedure, as laid down by the Local Government Act, 1933, is for one-third of the district councillors to retire each year, as in the case of boroughs. If, however, the district council, by a two-thirds majority, asks the county council, and the county council agrees, to make an order requiring the whole of the district councillors to retire together every third year, the district council is then subject to triennial general elections for all its members instead of to annual elections for one-third of its members.

The size of a council varies according to a number of circumstances. In the case of parish councils the number of councillors is to be from five to twenty-one as may be fixed by the county council. In the case of other councils no rule appears to be laid down. They vary in number from about fifteen to 150 or more. Population and rateable value are among the circumstances which are taken into account. Another circumstance is the fact that in all boroughs outside London, and in many urban and rural districts, the number of councillors should be divisible by three so as to fit in with the arrangement whereby one-third of the councillors retire each year. Where a borough or county district is divided into smaller areas – wards or parishes – for electoral purposes, the arrangement is that, as far as possible, one-third of the councillors for each electoral division shall retire annually. Where this system is in operation, therefore, the number of councillors for each division should be divisible by three. Then there is the fact that the county and borough aldermen must be equal in number to one-third of the councillors in counties and boroughs outside London, and equal in number to one-sixth of the councillors in the London County Council and the metropolitan boroughs.

Then there are the limiting factors that too small a council, or too large a council, is unworkable. A council of only a few members may degenerate into a hole and corner affair; moreover, it may not be big enough to provide sufficient members for the various committees which local authorities have to appoint. On the other hand a council much bigger than 150 members is too large for convenient working, as the council tends to lose its compactness as a local body.

A fair size for a borough, urban, or rural district council is about 30 to 40 members, for a county council 50 or 60, for a large county borough, such as Birmingham, about 150. The London County Council has 147 members including the aldermen. Some of the smaller non-county boroughs have councils with a total membership of no more than 15. The total membership of a metropolitan borough council may not exceed 71.

Qualification for election as councillor. Now supposing a person feels sufficiently imbued with public spirit to seek membership of a local council, what steps should he (or she) take? The position is legally the same for men and women. First of all a candidate for election to a local council must be a British subject, and of full age. Next, the candidate must have one of the following qualifications:

(*a*) Be a local government elector for the area of the local authority (i.e., be in the local electoral register); *or*

(*b*) own freehold or leasehold land within the area of the authority; *or*

(*c*) reside for twelve months previous to the election in the area of the authority (or, in the case of a parish council, within three miles of the parish).

In the case of a by-election to a parish council, the period of residence need only be since 25 March in the year next preceding the election. Parish council elections take place in

May, but, of course, by-elections may take place at any time of the year.

In addition to possessing the necessary qualification, the candidate must not be under any of the various legal disqualifications. These will be mentioned later in the chapter.

The election of councillors. The business of conducting a public election, whether for parliamentary or local government purposes, is a specialist's job and demands a very familiar acquaintance with a great number of complex and detailed requirements, as any registration officer or election agent will readily confirm. Heavy books have been written on the subject. It is not intended here to give more than an indication of the main outlines of the law and practice of local government elections.

Who are the electors? Registration. To be entitled to vote at a local government election, a person must be on the register of local government electors for the area in respect of which the election is being held.

The preparation of the register of electors is the business of the local registration officer. This officer has to keep a combined register of persons entitled to vote at parliamentary elections, and those entitled to vote at local elections. Very often the area of a parliamentary constituency is identical with that of a local government constituency. In those cases the registration officer for both parliamentary and local government elections is the same person; he will be the clerk of the county council, the town clerk of the borough, or the clerk of the urban district council. Where the two types of constituency intersect, one or other of these local clerks will be designated as registration officer. It is the duty of the registration officer to gather information and make due inquiry throughout the area as to the persons whose names ought to go on the electoral register.

Qualifications for registration. To get on the list, a person must have at least three qualifications, (i) be of full age; (ii) be a British subject; and (iii) have an interest in the area by way of residence, or the occupation or ownership of property.

A person may not be registered who is of unsound mind, or is serving a sentence of penal servitude, or imprisonment with hard labour, or of imprisonment (without hard labour) for a term exceeding twelve months. Nor may a person be registered who has been convicted of certain corrupt practices at elections; of such persons a list is kept by the registration officer and is published with the list of electors.

Being registered as a local government elector is, in itself, a qualification for election to membership of a local authority. It may therefore be of interest to add a note in explanation of the various qualifications for registration.

(i) *Full age.* Full age, both for men and women, is attained on the day preceding one's 21st birthday. A person must attain full age on or before the 'qualifying date' for registration (as to which see (iii) below).

(ii) *British subject.* A person may become a British subject by being born in any part of the British Empire, or by having a British father, by naturalization, or (in the case of a woman) by marrying a British subject. Citizens of the Republic of Ireland are treated as British subjects for registration purposes.

(iii) *Residence or property qualification.* In many respects the qualifications for parliamentary and local government electors are identical. If you have a vote at a parliamentary election, you are also entitled to a vote at a local government election. But there are certain qualifications which entitle you to vote at a local government election which do not entitle you to vote at a parliamentary election.

To get a vote at a local government election you (apart from qualifications (i) and (ii) above) must, on the qualifying date, reside in the constituency or occupy as owner or tenant any rateable land or premises of the yearly value of not less than £10.

The 'qualifying date', for any election taking place in the twelve months beginning with 16 February in any year, is 10 October in the previous year. A person who is not of full age on 10 October, but will be of age on the following 15 June, may be registered as an elector, but he may vote only if he is in fact of full age on the day of the poll.

The register is revised each year and published in February. Once on the register you remain entitled to vote during the currency of the register even though you have moved out of the constituency before the election actually takes place.

A person is not entitled to be registered as a voter for any one council more than once. Thus, in a county, he may own property in several county districts and may therefore be registered and vote for the council of any of those county districts. He may, however, be registered only once as an elector for the county council of that county; he must choose which constituency he will vote in, and the register will be marked accordingly.

Absent voters – Voting by proxy and by post. Members of the armed forces and persons in the service of the Crown may be registered as 'service voters' and can be allowed to vote by proxy. Other persons whose employment or occupation prevents their going in person to the poll may also be allowed to vote by proxy if they are likely to be out of the country on the day of the poll. The appointment of a proxy must be made in accordance with certain formalities; application must be made to the local registration officer.

A person who is unlikely to be able to go to the poll in

person, by reason of physical incapacity or of his employment or occupation, may apply to the registration officer to be registered as an absent voter, and may then vote by post at elections for county, borough, and urban district elections (but not for rural district or parish council elections).

How does an election start? Some little time before an election is due, the returning officer gives public notice of the day on which the election will be held. In the case of the ordinary annual or triennial elections, the day of election is fixed by law within certain limits.

General elections of county councillors are held early in April, and general elections for other councils are held early in May. The actual date is fixed by the Home Secretary for borough elections, and by the local county council for all other elections in the county.

In the case of a by-election for a casual vacancy, the day of election is fixed by the county returning officer (in the case of a county council), by the mayor (in the case of a borough outside London), by the clerk of the council (in the case of an election for an urban or rural district council, or by the town clerk (in the case of a metropolitan borough).

A casual vacancy in a parish council is filled by the parish council itself electing someone; there is no by-election.

Nomination. Now having assured yourself, by interview with the local officials, if you are in doubt, that you have the requisite qualification for election, what should you do next? You must get nominated. It is the duty of the returning officer (who is usually the mayor of the borough, or, in the case of other councils, the clerk of the council), to issue nomination papers as may be required. You must then get two electors of the area to propose and second you by signing the nomination paper. Further, if the election is for a county council, borough council outside London, or an urban district council, you must get eight other electors to support your nomination by signing the paper as well. In the case of rural district, metropolitan borough, or parish council elections the proposer and seconder alone are sufficient. If you are being put up as a party candidate, the party members will see to all this. If you are putting up for election on your own, this nomination business entails, as can be seen, quite a little trouble. Moreover, there are pitfalls. There are close restrictions as to the signing of these nomination papers. A safe rule to follow is that no elector should sign more than one nomination paper; instructions are, however, usually provided with the forms. You cannot be a candidate in more than one constituency at the same time.

One fact may console you for having to go to all this trouble. At a parliamentary election a candidate has to deposit £150, which he forfeits if he does not secure at the election more than an eighth of the votes polled. At a local government election there is no deposit required. Even if your proposer and seconder and the eight supporters to your nomination desert you at the last, and you poll no vote but your own, you lose nothing except your trouble.

The nomination paper must be delivered by the proper time on the appointed day. But delivery of the nomination paper alone is not enough to secure nomination. The candidate himself must send in before the last day for nominations, his own written consent to nomination. This written consent must be attested by one witness.

All this is to ensure that a candidate is really serious. If, however, the candidate changes his mind, he can, up to the twelfth day before the election is due to take place, withdraw his nomination, by written notice attested by one witness.

Uncontested election. The returning officer will scrutinize all these documents to see that they are in order. If the number of valid and unwithdrawn nominations does not exceed the number of members to be elected, the election is uncontested. All that the returning officer has to do is to publish on the day of election the list of names of the candidates. They are deemed to be duly elected – returned unopposed.

Contested election. If, however, the number of nominations is greater than the number of seats to be filled, then a contested election must be held. The election proceeds in the same way as a parliamentary election, with secret ballot. It is the job of the returning officer to get the ballot papers printed, arrange the polling stations, make provision for counting the votes, appoint the necessary clerks and presiding officers, and generally see to the conduct of the election. All this is done at the public cost, and involves the candidate in no expense.

Candidate's expenses. There are, however, various expenses which a candidate finds it almost inevitably necessary to incur. The hiring of halls for public meetings to address the electors, the printing of an election address and its delivery to all the electors, the printing and display of election posters, all involve the candidate in personal expense. With a view to placing all candidates on some sort of equality in their approach to the electorate, the law fixes very strict limits to the amount of money which a candidate may spend on his election to any type of council. His accounts have to be properly kept, and are open to close scrutiny after the election. The permitted expenses depend on the number of electors in the electoral area. Up to the first 500 electors the limit is £25. After that, the candidate may spend 2*d.* for each elector over the 500. Where there are two joint candidates, the maximum amount is reduced for each candidate by one fourth, and if there are more than two joint candidates, by one third. These expenses may be incurred in hiring committee rooms, engaging polling agents, and in printing, postage, and in the holding of meetings. After the election a proper return of the expenditure incurred must be sent to the clerk of the appropriate local authority.

Corrupt and illegal practices. Failure to keep within the permitted limits of expenditure, or to make a proper return, is an 'illegal practice' and is visited with penalties. Moreover, at all elections (whether the permitted limit is exceeded or not) there are certain expenses which should not be incurred and certain things which may not be done in any event.

Although you may lawfully get your friend to lend his car (free of charge) to bring electors to the poll, you must not hire a car for this purpose. You must not hire a band or orchestra to enliven the proceedings and attract electors. You must not buy banners or badges for your supporters, or furnish them with torches for a torchlight procession. They can, of course, supply their own equipment for all these purposes at their own expense. You must not give money to induce a person to vote or to abstain from voting. Nor may you offer gifts or employment for a like purpose. You may not do any treating by way of drink, food, or entertainment, other than normal hospitality.

At the same time the law forbids the use of threats or of force to influence voting, personation (that is, pretending to be someone else and using his vote) and making false declarations in connexion with an election.

The commission of these offences by a candidate or his supporters may result in the whole election being set aside. Proceedings may be taken in the courts for that purpose. At the same time the commission of any of these 'corrupt or illegal practices' by a candidate may disqualify him, for a period of from five to seven years according to circumstances, from voting at any local election, or from being elected to any local council, in addition to fines and imprisonment.

The poll. On polling day, within the hours fixed for voting, the electors make their choice. An elector who cannot read, or cannot register his vote himself through some physical cause, may ask the presiding officer at the polling station to record a vote on the elector's behalf. A blind elector may bring a companion to do the voting for him. Where, as is often the case, elections for rural district and parish councils are held together on the same day, the same ballot boxes may be used.

When the poll closes the ballot boxes are all taken under police protection to the place for counting the votes.

The count. The counting of the votes is one of the most critical proceedings at an election. The returning officer opens the ballot boxes in the presence of the candidates and their counting agents. These counting agents act as scrutineers over the persons who actually do the counting of the votes. The ballot papers are first counted to find out the total number of them. Then they are all mixed up together again, and the returning officer's staff begin to count up the votes received by each candidate. When there is only one vacancy the job is fairly easy. Each elector has only one vote in that case, and the counting is done by sorting out the ballot papers in a pile for each candidate. They are bundled up into fifties and stacked up under the eye of the returning officer.

When there are several vacancies the counting is rather more tricky. There may be, say, six vacancies, and 12 or 18 candidates. Each elector has six votes, one for each vacancy. Each elector can therefore give a vote to any six candidates; he may not give more than one vote to any one candidate. He may, if he likes 'plump' for one candidate by giving a vote to that candidate only, and not give a vote to anyone else. This will virtually increase the number of individual votes received by that candidate. Or the elector need only vote for five, or three candidates, giving one vote to each, and no more. If the elector votes for more candidates than there are vacancies, if, for instance, where there are six vacancies the elector marks seven votes or more on his ballot paper, the whole of the ballot paper is void.

The usual way of counting votes in the case of multiple vacancies is for one person to call out the names marked on each ballot paper, and for an assistant to make the votes on to a list. The marks on this list are then duly counted.

At the time this counting is going on, the candidates' counting agents or scrutineers are watching to ensure that everything is fairly done.

Any ballot paper that is open to question, as where the mark is not clear, or more votes have been marked on it than should have been, is set aside for the decision of the returning officer. It is astonishing how silly some people can be when performing the simple act of marking a voting paper. When there are, say, 18 candidates for 6 vacancies, some people mark their ballot paper with a vote for each candidate – 18 in all. Some don't seem to be able to put the vote in the right place; they put the cross in the margin instead of in the space provided, or they put the mark exactly on the lines between two spaces. Some people write encouraging or obscene remarks on their ballot papers; some people do not even mark their ballot papers at all! In all these cases the returning officer has to adjudicate, and give his decision as to the vote cast. When all the counting is done, he announces the result. Applause and speeches usually follow.

If there is exact equality of votes, any candidate may ask for a recount and, if there is still equality of votes, the returning officer determines the election by lot, e.g., by tossing up for it.

On a recount, however, as may well be supposed, the result generally turns out to be different from what it was on the former count. For that reason a candidate who appears on the first count to have lost the election by a very small margin nearly always presses the returning officer to order a recount. After the result has once been declared by the returning officer, no recount can take place except by order of the Court.

Date of entering office. If you have been elected a member of a county council or a borough council your membership starts on the fourth day after the election. The old councillors retire on the same day.

In the case of urban and rural district councils, and parish councils, the outgoing councillors retire on 20 May and the newly elected councillors take office on the same day.

These dates do not apply of course where a casual vacancy has arisen, as in the case of the death of a member. There will be in those cases an interval of a month or so (during which the election machinery will be put into operation) between the date of the vacancy and the date of the by-election. The new member takes up his membership as soon as the by-election is completed.

Acceptance of office. Even after all this, the formalities to be complied with are not over. The law seems anxious to make quite sure that when a person seeks membership of a local authority, he is really genuine in his intention.

Apart from the process of signifying his consent to nomination, and going through the test of a public election, the intending member, after election, must formally signify his acceptance of office. This must be done on a proper form

77

and delivered to the clerk of the authority. If the newly elected member fails to do this within two months of his election, his membership becomes vacant.

The statutory meeting of the authority. All local government authorities must hold every year an annual meeting and at least three other meetings. The annual meeting (or statutory meeting as it is often called) has to be held on a prescribed date shortly after the time of the year at which the general elections are held. At this statutory meeting certain business has to be transacted. The first business is the election of a new chairman or mayor. The next business in the case of county councils and boroughs must be the election of any aldermen, that is, of course, if it happens to be a year in which some of the aldermen end their term of office.

At the statutory meeting the council usually appoints its committees. It will also appoint a vice-chairman if necessary. In the case of a borough which appoints its own sheriff, this officer is also appointed at the annual meeting.

Election of chairman or mayor. The only persons who may vote for the chairman or mayor are members of the council. Outgoing aldermen must not, in their capacity as aldermen, vote in the election of the chairman. An outgoing alderman may have got himself elected at the recent general election as a councillor, in which case he may vote, as a newly elected councillor, for the chairman or mayor. Until the new chairman or mayor has been elected, the outgoing chairman or mayor presides. If there is equality of votes the person presiding at the meeting at which the election takes place has a casting vote, whether or not he was entitled to vote in the first instance. The new chairman or mayor must make a declaration of acceptance of this office.

Election of aldermen. Aldermen are elected by the councillors. No alderman may, as such, vote in the election of aldermen. Each councillor votes by signing and delivering to the chairman of the meeting a voting paper with the names of the persons voted for. Every councillor has a vote for each vacancy. Formal proposing and seconding is not required.

If a councillor is elected an alderman, he ceases to be a councillor. That means that a vacancy arises among the councillors, and a by-election must be held. The person presiding at the meeting has, in the case of equality of votes, a casting vote. Aldermen when elected must sign a declaration of acceptance of office. The aldermen do not sit in a separate chamber. They share all the proceedings of the council with the councillors and in the course of the business of the council are indistinguishable from them.

Disqualifications for being a member of a local authority. Even though the great voice of public opinion, exercised through the popular vote, may have favoured your election to the local council, you cannot remain a member if you have certain disqualifications. These disqualifications make it not only illegal for you to be elected, but an offence for you to act as a member after your election. The disqualifications are imposed by law with a view to keeping local government incorrupt and from becoming a profit-making career.

Holding a paid office, etc. If you hold any paid office or other place of profit in the gift or disposal of the local authority, you cannot lawfully be a member of that authority. Teachers in schools aided financially by the local authority, coroners whose salaries are paid by the local authority, recorders, are all disqualified for becoming members of the local authority. But a chairman or a mayor who is paid a salary for acting in that capacity is not disqualified; nor is the sheriff of a borough debarred from being a member of the borough council.

The law is so interested in keeping local government free from profit that provision has been made preventing a person who has been a member of a local authority from being appointed to any paid office under that authority until at least twelve months has elapsed since his ceasing to be a member.

The provisions applicable to the London County Council go even further and prohibit a person from being a member of the Council if and so long as he has directly or indirectly by himself or his partner any share or interest in any contract with the Council. This does not, however, prevent his renting a house from the Council or from entering into certain other specified contracts.

Bankruptcy. A person who has been adjudged bankrupt, or who has made a composition with his creditors, is disqualified from being a member of a local authority. This disqualification ceases five years after discharge, or earlier according to special circumstances.

Poor relief. Formerly you could not become a member of any local authority while you were in receipt of public assistance by way of out-relief or for twelve months thereafter, but the abolition of the Poor Law has now removed this disqualification. Receipt of national assistance or of medical aid through the National Health Service is no disqualification.

Offences. A sentence in the United Kingdom of imprisonment for not less than three months without the option of a fine renders the convicted person disqualified for five years from being a member of a local authority. Surcharge by the district auditor (as to which see Chapter 7) for a sum exceeding £500 operates as a similar disqualification. The commission of corrupt and illegal practices, as previously indicated, also creates a disqualification.

Failure to attend meetings. Apart from all these, a person may lose his membership of a local authority by ceasing to possess the qualifications required as indicated earlier in this chapter. Further a person may be debarred from membership if he fails to attend meetings for a period of six consecutive months, unless his absence was due to a reason approved by the council or was due to service in the armed forces.

If the mayor of a borough outside London is continuously absent from his borough, except in the case of illness, for a period exceeding two months, he ceases to be mayor.

The above-mentioned disqualifications also prohibit a person from being a member of a committee of the local authority.

Proceedings against persons wrongly acting as members. If any local government elector in the area of the local authority concerned finds out that a person has been acting as a member of the local authority when that person (a) was not properly qualified to be a member, or (b) was disqualified from being a member, or (c) has failed to make the proper declaration of acceptance of office, or (d) has resigned, or (e) has failed to attend meetings for six months without proper reason, or (f) has been elected but the election has been set aside by the court, the elector may take legal proceedings against the person who so acted as a member. Similar proceedings may be taken against a mayor who goes on acting as mayor after he has lost his office by reason of absence from the borough.

These proceedings must be taken within six months of the committing of the offence. A fine up to £50 may be imposed on the offender for each occasion on which he acted while incapacitated.

The City of London Corporation. The local government organization of the City of London differs very considerably from that in other parts of the country, and provides a unique example of the medieval type of local municipal authority. The organization is governed largely by royal charters and private Acts of Parliament, and has remained almost untouched by the general legislation applying to local authorities.

The Corporation consists of the citizens and freemen of the City and is named 'The Mayor and Commonalty and Citizens of the City of London'. It has, of course, a common seal. The operations of the Corporation are carried out by means of three assemblies, the Court of Common Hall, the Court of Aldermen, and the Court of Common Council.

The Court of Common Hall meets twice a year. It consists of the Lord Mayor, aldermen, sheriffs, and such of the liverymen of the City Companies as are freemen of the City. These Companies originated in the medieval craft guilds. The liverymen are fully-fledged members entitled to wear the livery or costume of the craft of the Company. The freedom of the City can be conferred as an honour without fees, or can be obtained by apprentices or children of freemen and ratepayers, on payment of fees.

The Court of Common Hall elects the two City Sheriffs, and certain other officers, and nominates two aldermen for the office of Lord Mayor from among those who have been sheriffs. Voting is by show of hands; but a poll may be demanded, and the election will then proceed in modern style.

The Court of Aldermen consists of the Lord Mayor and aldermen. Each ward of the City has one alderman. There are twenty-six in all; the Lord Mayor is one. Each alderman is elected for life, by the local government electors. The election is called a 'wardmote'. The franchise is somewhat similar to that applicable in other local government elections. Qualifications and disqualifications for aldermanship are similar to those applying to be aldermen in boroughs and counties. Each city alderman is a justice of the peace. The court sits as a court of law for the trial of minor offences. It appoints the Recorder of London, and governs the city police. It appoints, from the two aldermen nominated by the Court of Common Hall, the Lord Mayor for the ensuing year.

The Court of Common Council consists of the Lord Mayor, aldermen, and 159 common councilmen. These latter are elected by the local electors by public election (wardmotes) conducted under similar provisions to those applicable to other elections. The qualifications and disqualifications are also somewhat similar to those of county and borough councillors. The Court of Common Council is virtually the local government authority for the City and carries out functions similar to those of other local authorities.

The Lord Mayor, having been elected by the Court of Common Hall and the Court of Aldermen, is presented to the Lord Chancellor for the Sovereign's approval. He is then sworn in by the Judges of the High Court. This is the occasion for the annual procession and Lord Mayor's Show. The Lord Mayor presides over the proceedings of the Courts of Common Hall, Aldermen, and Common Council, and has various ancient offices, duties, and privileges.

The area of the City of London is about one square mile, and its resident population is about 5000, although the electorate, being largely occupiers of business premises, numbers about 15,000 (1958 figures). The City's functions as a local government authority are relatively small in comparison with its great prestige. Apart from income from rates, the Corporation has a very substantial income from private property. This private income is spent for public purposes, on charitable and educational endowments, the maintenance of the City Courts of Justice, open spaces, including Burnham Beeches and Epping Forest, and in the entertainment of foreign and other distinguished visitors.

CHAPTER 4

WHAT LOCAL AUTHORITIES DO

Distribution of Functions between Local Authorities

Conferment of powers. Local government authorities come into existence in one of three ways, (i) by royal charter, (ii) by Act of Parliament, or (iii) by a Minister's Order confirmed by Parliament. To find out the functions of a local authority, you must look at its charter or the Order or the Acts of Parliament which govern it.

A body which is created by charter has all the powers of an ordinary person, except in so far as those powers are altered by the charter itself or by Act of Parliament. A charter is the traditional method of creation of a borough. None the less, for the most part, the powers and duties of boroughs so created are, like those of all other types of local authority, dependent upon Acts of Parliament.

The need for powers. Modern local government is concerned largely with the carrying on of public services which are financed out of rates and taxes. It is one of the first principles of British constitutional law that no person shall be taxed, or rated, without his consent or the authority of Parliament. Accordingly, without specific parliamentary sanction, a local authority would be in a difficulty in attempting to carry on its public services. It could not levy rates, or spend public money. Moreover, Parliament has in many cases imposed a direct duty upon local authorities to exercise functions. Under the Education Act, 1944, for instance, county councils and county borough councils are under an obligation to provide sufficient schools for their areas.

85

Further, there are a number of services, such as the regulation of buildings, the making of by-laws, the licensing of cinemas, concert halls, and dance halls, and the making and enforcement of town-planning schemes, which in one way or another interfere with the private rights or property of individual citizens. Here again it is, because of that interference, necessary that the local authority should have sanction from Parliament to enable the authority lawfully to carry out its duties.

The powers and duties of all types of local authority are in almost every way defined, described, limited, imposed, or affected by Acts of Parliament. If you want to find out what an authority may or may not do, you must look at the various Acts of Parliament concerning that authority.

Obligatory and permissive powers. When Parliament has decided that local public services, such as public education, or the testing of weights and measures, shall be provided, it is the general rule for an Act to be passed describing what is to be done, and stating what the duties of local authorities are to be, and what classes of local authority are to have those duties.

In other cases, Parliament by Act imposes a duty on the public in general, and requires certain classes of local authority to see to the enforcement of that duty. For instance, the legislation relating to shops lays down certain requirements to be observed by shopkeepers in the matter of closing hours, holidays to the staff, and hours of work. Under that legislation the local authorities have to see that the requirements of the law are complied with.

Sometimes the powers conferred on local authorities are permissive, that is to say, the local authority may do certain things if it thinks fit, or if there is a local need for them. Local authorities are, for example, empowered to provide buildings for carrying out their business. The power is there, given by Parliament, but there is no obligation upon the local authority to exercise the power. There is no need to have a town hall or county hall if the council doesn't want one; the aldermen and councillors can sit and transact their business in the open air, under a tree, as their Saxon fore-fathers did – that is, if they want to, and are willing to put up with the inconvenience. The power to provide official buildings is permissive, not obligatory.

The powers of a local authority are not identical with its duties; in other words, the list of things it can do (if it likes) is different from the list of things it must do (whether it likes to or not).

Local variations in powers and duties. Although it is quite easy to indicate broadly what local authorities do, and the various services which are carried on by them, it is by no means easy to describe exactly what functions each individual local authority has. The powers and duties vary with local circumstances. Some borough councils have many more powers than others. The same applies to county councils and district councils. The functions of each type of authority are so numerous and varied, and differ in each locality to such an extent that, if you were to ask any town clerk to give you a complete list of the powers and duties of his council, you would be asking him to do a fairly lengthy job. Without help from the authority itself, an ordinary member of the public would have to undertake a very difficult and detailed inquiry in order to ascertain what are the complete powers and duties of any particular local authority.

Variations according to status. The powers of local authorities vary, first of all, according to the class to which the authority belongs. It is easy to appreciate that the councils of county boroughs, which are all-purpose authorities and are responsible for all the local government services within the boroughs, have a somewhat wider range of functions than county councils, who share the work of local government with the non-county borough councils, the urban and rural district councils, and the parish councils. But even as between individual county borough councils there are differences in the powers and duties to be performed. County councils have individual differences too.

In the case of non-county borough councils and urban district councils, there are differences between authorities of the same class according to the population of the borough or district. If the population is above a certain size, the borough or district council has more powers than in a similar area with less population. This, of course, has an effect on the distribution of functions as between the borough and district councils and the county council.

But the differences between the powers and duties of local government authorities do not depend only on the type of the authority or the population. Differences in function may arise for other reasons.

Local Acts of Parliament. Every local authority, other than a parish council, may ask Parliament to confer special powers upon the local authority. Parliament very often does this by what is known as a Private Act, or Local Act. Such an Act is applicable only to the individual local authority to which the Act refers. Some local authorities have very many Acts of this kind. The London County Council for instance has made an almost annual practice of asking Parliament for special powers. As a result, the Council has over 100 Private Acts, giving powers to the Council for its own particular purposes or to meet special needs. Most of the other large local authorities also have Private Acts, and so have many of the smaller authorities.

Some of these Acts relate to the carrying out of works, such as the laying of sewers, road widenings, and other similar operations which involve interference with private property or necessitate the compulsory purchase of property by the council. Other Acts give powers to the local council to meet particular requirements of the locality. At one time the pigeons in London, around Trafalgar Square, St Paul's Churchyard, and other places, became so numerous that they developed into a real nuisance, and the City Corporation and the Metropolitan Borough Councils obtained powers from Parliament to deal with them.

Sometimes a local authority may wish to conduct a particular enterprise such as a municipal bank; for such a purpose a Private Bill will be sought. Similarly, it may be desired to control certain businesses or activities such as employment agencies, fun fairs, or street trading, which, if not suitably regulated, might become a public nuisance or be otherwise undesirable. Powers to deal with such matters have been conferred on a number of individual local authorities by Private Acts. You cannot therefore make up a complete list of what your local council can lawfully do, without finding out if it has any Private Acts of Parliament, and, if so, what powers are conferred by those Acts.

Adoptive Acts. One of the principal objects in having a local government system is to let local representative opinion decide (within limits) how best to meet local needs and local conditions. Accordingly, in some matters, Parliament has by Act prescribed certain powers which local authorities can take upon themselves, if they so desire, subject to conditions which Parliament has laid down. Examples of this type of legislation have been provided by the Public Libraries

Acts and the Baths and Washhouses Acts, under which local authorities of the classes mentioned in the Acts were enabled formally to decide to accept the powers to provide public libraries, or public baths, on the conditions laid down in the Acts. Such Acts of Parliament are known as 'Adoptive Acts'. The fact that one authority may choose to adopt the powers of such Acts, while a neighbouring authority does not choose to do so, still further accounts for the difference between the powers and duties of individual local authorities throughout the country.

Transfer of powers. Delegation and surrender of powers. It is provided in some Acts of Parliament that, in the first instance, the local authorities for the purpose of carrying out the powers and duties of the Act shall be authorities of a certain class, but that those authorities may, if they so wish, pass their powers over to an authority of another class. For instance, in the Housing Act, 1957, it is provided that the housing authorities shall be the councils of county boroughs and county districts; but that the council of a rural district may, by agreement with the county council, allow the county council to exercise all or any of the district council's powers to provide housing accommodation. This is a case where the lesser authority may surrender its powers to a greater authority.

The Shops Act, 1950, which deals with the conditions of employment of shop assistants and the closing hours for shops, gives to county councils certain powers of enforcing the Act, but provides that the county council may, if it so wishes, delegate to a rural or urban district council, on agreed terms, the county council's powers under the Act. This is a case where powers may be transferred from a great authority to a lesser.

In the two instances mentioned, it is impossible, without

making particular inquiry in each locality, to know which local authority in the area has provided the housing, or which council has the duty of enforcing the requirements relating to shops.

Delegation of health and welfare functions. Under the Local Government Act, 1948, in areas outside Greater London, the council of a non-county borough, urban district, or rural district with a population of 60,000 or more (or with less, if the Minister of Health agrees) can request that the county council shall delegate certain of its functions to the borough or district council. The functions are those relating to the care of mothers and babies; health visiting; home nursing; vaccination and immunization; home helps, the prevention of illness and the care and after-care of sick persons; the provision of welfare arrangements for blind and disabled persons; and the regulation of nurseries and child minders.

A council wishing to take over these functions by delegation must make a scheme, in cooperation with the county council. The scheme will prescribe the conditions under which the delegated functions are to be exercised on the county council's behalf, and will deal with matters of accounting and finance, including the manner in which the county council are to reimburse the borough or district council.

The scheme must be approved by the Minister of Health. In exceptional circumstances, with the Minister's approval, the scheme can also provide for the delegation of functions relating to the provision of residential or temporary accommodation for aged, infirm, or other persons in need, and the provision of care and after-care of mentally afflicted persons in residential accommodation. There is provision for the revocation and, at prescribed intervals, for the variation of schemes.

Delegation of education functions. Under the Education Act, 1944, the council of each county other than London is required, with the approval of the Minister of Education, to make a scheme for dividing the county into divisions, and to constitute for each division a body of persons, with knowledge of local education needs and circumstances, called a 'divisional executive', for carrying out on behalf of the county council education functions as defined in the scheme.

Where the population of a non-county borough or urban district is 60,000 or more (or less where there are exceptional circumstances) the borough or district council may claim its area to be an 'excepted district' and to have its own scheme of divisional administration.

Apart from such provisions in particular Acts permitting the transfer of powers between local authorities, the Minister of Housing and Local Government has general powers to confer, by order, upon rural district councils the functions of urban district councils – a sort of promotion in status. He has also power to transfer to county councils and county borough councils, by provisional order subject to confirmation by Parliament, the functions of local public bodies such as conservators operating in the area of the county or borough.

Every county council outside London has general powers to delegate almost any of its functions to the council of a county district within the county; the council of a county district will, in such a case, operate the functions as agents for the county council.

The Minister of Housing and Local Government may also, by order, with the consent of the councils concerned, transfer powers as between the London County Council, the Common Council of the City of London, and the Metropolitan Borough Councils.

Joint Committees and Joint Boards. The distribution of local government functions in a particular area may be further complicated by the appointment of joint committees by local authorities, as mentioned in Chapter 2. Any local authority may combine with any other local authority in setting up a joint committee to carry out any of the functions of the local authorities. Joint committees have been appointed for town-planning purposes, or for providing certain medical services in areas insufficiently populous or wealthy to provide adequate separate services.

Joint Boards, as also explained in Chapter 2, may also be appointed in certain cases, as, for example, to provide water, cemeteries, sewerage, main drainage, or local health services.

General scope of local authorities' functions. For all the reasons stated above, it is not possible, without an indigestible and intolerable amount of detail, to indicate precisely what each authority does. The field of services is very wide, and the local differences between the functions of the various authorities make such a task unduly involved. The citizen who goes to his local town hall to make an inquiry or complaint must unfortunately and inevitably expect to be told that the matter in question is one to be raised in some other quarter. There are, however, certain broad general divisions of functions between the various types of local authority. It is proposed, with all these considerations in mind, to give now a brief review of the various services which local authorities are concerned with. The extent of the concern of each class of authority will generally not be shown, but, at the end of this chapter, lists will be given indicating, in a very general way, the distribution of the principal functions between the several classes of local government authority.

Services Provided by Local Authorities

(I) PUBLIC HEALTH

Public health services cover a very wide range, and include (*a*) services maintained to prevent ill-health, e.g. sanitary services such as the provision and inspection of drains and sewers, the suppression of nuisances likely to be injurious to health, and the inspection of food and drugs, (*b*) services for the promotion of health, e.g., the provision of baths and wash-houses, and maternity and child welfare services, and (*c*) services for the cure of ill-health, for example, the provision of clinics and treatment centres.

(*a*) Prevention

Sewerage and drainage. A sewer is a conduit which takes effluent from more than one house or property. Sewers may be private, i.e., constructed by an owner for his own use, or public, i.e., constructed or taken over by the local authority. Private drains and sewers must be maintained by the owner, subject to the requirements and supervision of the local authority. The local authority has power to supervise the sanitary arrangements in buildings, and may make and enforce by-laws for the purpose.

Where a building is 100 feet or less from a public sewer, the local authority may require the sewage from the building to be discharged into the public sewer. Hence, in built-up areas, the usual practice is for all sewage to be discharged into public sewers; but in rural areas, it is common for each house to have its own cess-pool or sewerage system. It is the duty of the local authority to make sufficient provision for the proper sewerage of the district. The local authority must also make proper arrangements for the disposal of sewage discharged into public sewers.

Trade effluents may also be discharged into public sewers by arrangement with the local authority.

A drain is a conduit leading from one house or property into a sewer. The term also includes channels and gratings for taking off surface water from roads and premises.

The sewerage arrangements are to some extent related to the arrangements for surface water drainage, in that the drainage is frequently discharged into public sewers. Land drainage for agricultural purposes is, however, in many areas, the concern of a local River Board or Land Drainage Board composed of representatives of local government authorities and other persons. Their business is to make necessary arrangements for the proper drainage of the land in their areas.

Local authorities, as part of their sanitary duties, have power to construct public conveniences and lavatories.

Watercourses and water supply. The law recognizes a general right on the part of owners of property along the banks of rivers and streams to the use and flow of the water. None the less, local authorities, on behalf of the public, have a duty to exercise control over watercourses for certain purposes.

In order to protect the purity of fishing streams, River Boards have powers of control.

It is illegal to pollute a river or stream by discharging refuse from manufacture, rubbish, sewage, or other noxious matter. Proceedings to enforce these provisions may be taken by a local authority.

Where a watercourse, well, pond, etc., is used for human water supply, the local authorities have power to close the source of supply if the water is contaminated.

In certain localities the supply of piped water to premises is undertaken by a local authority as a trading undertaking.

In other localities it is undertaken by private water companies.

Nuisances and offensive trades. Local authorities are obliged to employ sanitary inspectors to see that no health nuisances exist, e.g. from filthy premises or animals, from rubbish dumps, bad and insanitary conditions in factories and workshops, smoke pollution, contaminated water supply or watercourses, or unfenced quarries. The local authority may take proceedings to stop these and other such nuisances.

Certain trades and businesses likely to cause offensive smells or be harmful to public health may only be established or carried on subject to the consent and supervision of the local authority. Examples are blood boiler, bone boiler, fat extractor or melter, glue maker, soap boiler, tallow melter, tripe boiler, rag and bone dealer.

Public cleansing. Refuse collection. Local authorities may, and, when ordered to do so by the Minister of Housing and Local Government, must, regularly remove house refuse, and cleanse earth closets and cess-pools. They may require or provide (at a charge) regulation dustbins to be used for house refuse.

The authority may charge for removing trade refuse, and, in special circumstances, make a charge for cleansing earth closets, cess-pools, and the like.

Local authorities may water streets, and may undertake, or be compelled by the Minister to undertake, street sweeping and cleaning.

Persons or premises in a filthy, unwholesome, or verminous condition may be cleansed or disinfected by the local authority.

Food and drugs. Under the law relating to food and drugs, strict requirements are laid down as to purity generally and as to the quality and standards of certain foods such as milk, butter, margarine, bread, and flour. Precautions must be taken against contaminating food, as by proper packing and proper conditions of manufacture, storage, and sale.

Purveyors of milk must be registered. Slaughter-houses must be licensed. Cases of food poisoning must be notified. Suspected food must be investigated. Markets are subject to inspection. To ensure that all these requirements are complied with, local authorities appoint inspectors. Samples of food and drugs may be taken for investigation by a public analyst. Local authorities may provide means for cleansing shell-fish, may establish their own municipal markets, slaughter-houses, cold air stores, and refrigerators, and may make by-laws on various matters relating to the handling of food and drugs.

Infectious diseases, notification and disinfection. Local authorities have, subject to regulations made by the Minister of Health, considerable powers to prevent the spread of infectious diseases. Cases of 'notifiable disease' must be notified to the local medical officer of health. The list of such diseases may be varied according to circumstances. Persons suffering from such diseases may be compulsorily removed to hospital unless properly isolated at home. Temporary accommodation for the families of infected persons may be provided. Premises, clothing, bedding, etc., may be disinfected by the local authority. Home nursing may be provided.

Vaccination. Local authorities must provide vaccination free of charge within six months of birth for all children whose parents do not make a conscientious objection.

(b) Promotion of health

Baths and wash-houses. Public baths for personal cleansing, swimming baths, and bathing places may be established by local authorities. The swimming baths may be let for public functions. Wash-houses, where housewives may, for a reasonable charge, take their household laundry and wash it at the municipal wash-tubs, with adequate hot water and boiling facilities, may also be established.

Maternity and child welfare. With a view to safeguarding the health of the future population, local authorities are empowered to set up maternity homes and clinics where ante-natal and post-natal advice, treatment, and assistance may be obtained whether free or at charges to suit the income of the recipient. Child welfare work may continue until the child reaches school age, after which the child passes into the scope of the school medical service provided by the local education authorities.

All births in a local authority's area must be notified to the local medical officer of health, so that he or his health visitors may be in a position to offer help and advice. Education in parent-craft may be given, and domestic help in the home to expectant and nursing mothers may be provided.

Midwives. It is the duty of local authorities to ensure that a suitable number of qualified midwives is available in each area, either by the local authority itself employing midwives, or by making suitable arrangements with voluntary organizations.

Child life protection. Child welfare authorities are also required to concern themselves with the supervision of persons undertaking the nursing or maintenance of children for reward (foster parents). Local authorities have also responsibility for the care and protection of children deprived of a normal home life.

(c) Cure of ill-health

Clinics and health centres. An important integral part of the
National Health Service is the establishment of hospitals
and other centres for medical treatment. A large number of
hospitals, sanatoria, and convalescent homes were formerly
provided by the larger local authorities, or by combinations
of smaller authorities through a joint board or joint committee. Minor authorities acting alone often provided local
dispensaries or clinics for various forms of out-patient
treatment.

The arrangements for dealing, under special legislation,
with maternity and child welfare, tuberculosis, venereal
diseases, and notifiable infectious diseases were interwoven
with general hospital and medical services, and with the
medical treatment of sick persons under the old poor law. As
health services developed, there was need for continuous co-
ordination and adjustment of the various health functions
of the authorities. A special hospital or centre to deal with
one type of disease needs to cater for a fairly large area so
that the number of prospective patients may be sufficient to
justify the special arrangements. On the other hand, a
general hospital to deal with ordinary complaints, street
accidents, and maternity cases need not cover so large an
area; for there is usually plenty of that sort of case every-
where. It was for such reasons among others that hospitals
have now been taken over by the central government and
are managed by Regional Boards and Hospital Management
Committees. County and county borough councils are 'local
health authorities' and provide maternity and child welfare
clinics and day nurseries. These authorities are also to provide health centres where doctors can engage in group practice and where instruction on health matters can be given.

Ambulance services are provided by local authorities, not only to pick up the victims of street accidents, but also to convey patients to and from their homes and the hospitals.

As an incident to these medical services, local health authorities provide home nursing, after care, and domestic help.

Private nursing homes. These must all be registered with a local authority. As a condition of registration, requirements are usually imposed with a view to ensuring that the nursing home is safe and suitable and properly conducted.

Local welfare service. County and county borough councils are required to provide a local welfare service for the blind and disabled. Training at centres and workshops is undertaken, and provision is made for employment. Charges may be made for these services. Home visitors are appointed to keep in touch with afflicted persons in their homes.

(II) HOUSING, TOWN PLANNING, BUILDING, PARKS

Housing. It is not by medical action alone or with the usual sanitary safeguards that the physical well-being of the public can be secured. The health of the people depends upon proper housing conditions. Accordingly, as a service somewhat allied to public health, local authorities have been given functions in relation to the housing needs of the people. Originally these functions were closely restricted to the provision of housing for the working classes; but the powers of local authorities now include the provision of housing for other classes. The acute shortage of houses due to the second world war made it necessary to empower local authorities to undertake the repair of war-damaged houses irrespective of what class of person the houses were for, and to cooperate in the provision of temporary houses for persons, whatever their class, who needed accommodation.

Between the two world wars the housing activity of local authorities was tremendous. The powers were exercisable both within and without the area of the individual local authority. On the outskirts of our large towns huge housing estates, built and managed by local authorities, have been established. The power to provide housing includes power to build necessary shops and other buildings for the use of the inhabitants of the estate. The housing may be by way of blocks of flats, or terrace or cottage types.

Slum clearance. In areas where the housing is unfit for human habitation or injurious to health, two courses may be taken by a local authority. It can define the area on a map, and declare the area to be a 'clearance area', and, after due notice to owners (who have certain rights of objection to the Minister of Housing and Local Government, whose duty is to ensure that the action of the local authority is properly taken) the authority may either order the owners to clear away the bad buildings, or may buy the land in the area and demolish the buildings thereon.

Compensation is not paid for bad buildings demolished, but is paid for any sites purchased by the local authority, and is also paid for any good buildings which have to be demolished to enable a proper rebuilding scheme to be undertaken.

As an alternative to clearing the area the local authority may declare the area to be a 're-development area', and submit re-development plans to the Minister. Alternatively, the owners of land in the area may themselves submit to the local authority schemes for re-development to be undertaken by the owners themselves. If the local authority approves the owner's schemes, the authority must leave the re-development to the owners.

Somewhat similar powers of purchase and reconstruction are given to local authorities under the town-planning law in respect of areas which have been war-damaged (see below).

Overcrowding. Local authorities have a duty to make surveys of their areas with a view to seeing what over-crowding exists. Legal action may be taken against owners and occupiers who permit overcrowding. The local authority must submit to the Minister proposals for abating the over-crowding by the provision of new houses.

Individual unfit houses. The law requires that all houses let for dwellings shall be fit for human habitation. Apart from making and enforcing by-laws relating to the condition of houses, local authorities must carry out inspections. Owners may be required by the local authority to do any needed repairs, or the house may be purchased and repaired by the authority or ordered to be demolished. Local authorities may give financial assistance to private owners to improve their houses.

Small dwellings acquisition. Powers have been conferred on local authorities to advance money on loan on very favourable terms to an intending purchaser of a small house who wants it for his own occupation. Considerable use has been made of these facilities.

Control of building. Local authorities have power to supervise and control the construction of dwelling houses and other buildings to ensure that they are properly and safely erected, have adequate space, are not unduly high, and have proper sanitary arrangements, water supply, and ventilation. By-laws are made for this purpose, and plans may be required to be submitted before building is commenced.

Dangerous structures and buildings may be suitably dealt with by a local authority.

Common lodging houses, etc. Common lodging houses must be registered with a local authority, and be conducted subject to the requirements of the authority.

Canal boats used for human habitation are subject to similar provisions.

Tents, sheds, vans, and caravans used as dwellings, and camping sites may also be controlled by local authorities by means of by-laws or by licences issued subject to conditions.

Town and country planning is a comparatively new local government service, but has attracted much attention, especially in view of the opportunities for planned reconstruction which war damage has provided in some localities. Unregulated development of property in the past has led to many deplorable results – indiscriminate mixing of housing and industry, insufficiency and maldistribution of open space, unsuitably designed streets, and general lack of appreciation of the fact that, although a town may be owned by many individuals as their private property, its external appearance and its efficiency as a town are matters of public concern.

In addition to regulating the actual construction and design of buildings, local planning authorities may control the use to which buildings are put and the manner in which sites are developed. The authority may divide up its area into zones for particular uses, e.g., residential, commercial, or industrial, and may prevent the intrusion into a zone of any but the type of building designated for that zone.

Land may be acquired compulsorily by an authority to enable the authority itself to carry out development. In the case of war-damaged areas, the local authorities' powers are designed to facilitate the development of the damaged area as a whole as a 'reconstruction area'. Somewhat similar powers are conferred in respect of areas of bad lay-out and obsolete development. Compensation is payable to owners whose land is compulsorily purchased, and, in certain cases, to owners whose property is adversely affected by town-planning operations.

Parks and open spaces. All local authorities have power to buy or accept gifts of land for parks, gardens, and open spaces. Disused burial grounds may also be used for these purposes. Local authorities have power to provide recreational facilities in parks, by way of swimming and paddling pools, music, and games. A local authority may, in some cases, buy land outside its own area for open space, and may cooperate with other local authorities for the purpose. The Green Belt which is being established around London is a result of cooperation of this kind.

(III) EDUCATION

Compulsory public education was first instituted in 1870 by the creation of school boards for providing elementary education. Since that time, tremendous developments in educational methods and education policy have taken place.

Under present law, county councils and county borough councils are under a duty to contribute towards the spiritual, moral, mental, and physical development of the community by securing that efficient education in their areas shall be available by way of primary education, secondary education and further education. Other local authorities are given an opportunity of taking a share in carrying out this important task.

Education no longer means instruction merely in reading, writing, and arithmetic. Regard must be had to religious and moral instruction, physical and vocational training, and health needs.

Parents are obliged to see that their children from 5 years of age onwards receive efficient full-time education suitable to the age, ability, and aptitude of the children, either by regular attendance at school or otherwise. The responsibility of making the necessary provision for this purpose is upon the local education authority.

The health and physical well-being of the children are to be looked after by regular medical inspection and treatment, by the provision of milk and meals and other refreshment, by the board and lodging of children in necessary cases, by the issue of clothing at charges to suit the parent's income, by the provision of facilities for recreation, and social and physical training, by the enforcement of cleanliness, and by the supply of transport where necessary to enable children to attend school.

Local authorities have power to control the employment of children and young persons, so that the full benefit of education may be gained. Scholarships to universities, public schools, and other establishments may be arranged. No fees for the education given are to be charged to pupils in schools and colleges provided by local education authorities, but fees at rates suited to the purse of the parents may be charged for the board, lodging, and other provision made beyond the education itself.

Side by side with this state system of education, administered by local authorities under the supervision of the Ministry of Education, are the private, voluntary (denominational), and independent ('public') schools, colleges, and universities, all charging their own fees. Some of these establishments may be aided by grant from the government, and local education authorities may enter into arrangements with them as may be necessary, with a view to meeting the educational needs of the area.

Necessary arrangements must be made for the education, in special schools, of blind and deaf children, and for those otherwise physically or mentally defective. Trade and vocational education is to be provided. Evening and part-time instruction must be arranged for persons over school age.

When to all these duties is added the obligation to ensure that sufficient teachers are recruited and trained, it will be appreciated that the work of local education authorities is very considerable.

(IV) AGE AND INDIGENCE

It is part of the law of this country that no one must unwillingly starve or be without necessary shelter. For centuries there has (more or less) been some sort of provision for the relief of the poor. The administration has undergone many reforms. The Poor Law which had, since the time of Queen Elizabeth I, provided for the relief of poverty by local authorities is now abolished. The National Assistance Board makes money payments to poor persons. County and county borough councils provide residential accommodation for the aged and for persons in need of care and attention not otherwise available. Charges must be made for this service. Liable relatives may be required to contribute.

(V) HIGHWAYS AND BRIDGES

Road maintenance. The upkeep of public roads and bridges is the oldest of all the local government services, and has been the subject of many Acts of Parliament and legal disputes through the centuries.

Nowadays, outside the County of London, certain trunk

roads – roads of national character – are the responsibility of the Government. The maintenance of all other public roads is a duty placed on local authorities.

Private roads; New roads. Private roads, such as an entrance drive to a hotel, and places such as the forecourts to shops, petrol filling stations, cinemas, and other buildings are not repairable by the local authority as a matter of duty, although the public may have access to the road or forecourt. It is sometimes a matter of difficulty to decide whether a road or footway is public or not. It may become public by dedication by the owner. This may be presumed in certain cases from long use by the public. Or the owner can expressly dedicate it to the public by formally handing it over to the local authority.

Private roads may be repaired by the local authority where the local authority thinks it necessary, but the cost of repair is charged upon the owners of the land fronting on to the private road. A private road can, with certain formalities, be adopted by a local authority as a public road; indeed, the owners in certain circumstances may demand that the local authority shall take the road over. The local authority, before taking a private road over, must be satisfied that the road is properly made up. If the road is not made up to the satisfaction of the local authority, the authority, before taking it over, can do what work is necessary, and charge the frontagers each with a share of the cost. It is because of all this that, when houses are built on estates laid out by private developers, the purchasers of the houses are often required to pay 'road charges' for the making up of the new roads. The local authority may itself make a contribution towards the cost of making up the new roads. Once a road is adopted or taken over as a public road, it remains a public road for ever.

Road improvements. Local authorities may themselves

make new roads or make improvements, such as widenings in existing roads. In these cases the road is a public road from the outset and does not have to be formally taken over. The local authority which has power to make the improvement may not be the authority for maintenance. Hence, in these cases, after the completion of the works by the 'improvement authority', the road is handed over to the 'highway authority' for maintenance.

Classification of roads. The responsibilities as between local authorities for roads depend to a certain extent on the classification of the roads. 'County roads' are the concern of the county councils; local roads and streets in boroughs and urban districts are the concern of the borough and urban district councils. Rural district councils have less concern with roads.

Street lay-out, etc. As an incident to their powers to control building development, local authorities have powers of supervision over new streets laid out by private developers. The authorities can fix the lines of the streets, determine the width and levels, and may also settle the line of building frontage. Local authorities also have powers of street naming and numbering. In the case of main roads they have power to prevent 'ribbon development', by prohibiting building along the roads, and by restricting the access to the main roads from side roads. Powers also exist to control the planting of trees, to lop trees, to regulate the placing of lamp-posts, bins, bus stops, and shelters, and to deal with offences of obstruction and nuisance in relation to highways.

Bridges. Somewhat similar powers and duties are conferred on local authorities in respect of the construction and maintenance of bridges. Restrictions may be imposed as to the weight of traffic to be allowed to pass over the bridge. There are a number of bridges to which the public have access, which have been built, and are maintained, by such organizations as railway, harbour, and canal authorities.

(VI) POLICE

Police authorities. In counties the police force is maintained by a standing joint committee of county councillors and justices of the peace. In boroughs which have separate police forces, the police authority is a Watch Committee of the borough council. As to the Metropolitan Police, see Chapter 2. The City of London has its own police force. The police arrangements throughout the country are closely supervised and coordinated by the Home Office.

(VII) MISCELLANEOUS FUNCTIONS

Very many additional powers and duties have been given to local authorities according to national or local needs. Some of these functions are for the provision of public amenities, some are for the protection of the public, others take the form of necessary services, others are of the nature of public records.

(a) Amenities

Libraries, etc. Public lending or reference libraries and information bureaux may be provided, and museums and art galleries may be established.

Monuments. Fountains and water troughs may be erected, statues and war memorials may be maintained.

Wild birds protection. It is an offence to destroy certain wild birds and their eggs. Local authorities are concerned in the administration and enforcement of the law.

(b) Public protection

Explosives. Premises where explosives are stored and certain firework factories must be registered with or licensed by the local authorities. Local authorities may also provide magazines for storage.

Employment agencies. Theatrical employers, and agencies for theatrical employment must be registered with a local authority. Many local authorities have power to require domestic and other employment agencies to be registered or licensed, so that the local authority may impose conditions designed to secure that the agencies are properly conducted.

Fertilizers and feeding stuffs. These must comply with certain standards of purity and quality. Local authorities have power to enforce compliance and to make inspections and analysis.

Fire Brigade. Until 1941, local authorities were responsible for the organization and equipment of local fire brigades. This service was nationalized for war purposes by the formation of the National Fire Service. The service has now been transferred back to local authorities – the councils of counties and county boroughs.

Entertainments. Cinemas must be licensed by a local authority. In London and the Home Counties, premises for public music and dancing must be licensed by a local authority; in other parts of the country music and dancing licences are issued by the local justices of the peace (who also issue liquor licences). Theatres are licensed in some parts of London and certain other places by the Lord Chamberlain; in other parts of the country theatre licences are issued by a local authority. Racecourses and tracks must also be licensed by a local authority. The issue of any of these licences is usually subject to numerous conditions as to the safety and conduct of the premises.

Local authorities (other than parish authorities) may themselves provide entertainments of all kinds and provide premises for the purpose.

Petrol. Premises where petroleum is stored, and petrol filling stations, are subject to control by the local authority, by means of licences, by-laws, and regulations. Safety precautions are imposed and the appearance of petrol filling stations is regulated.

Shops. The laws relating to shops contain provisions to safeguard shop assistants. Hours of work, closing hours, holidays, Sunday work, meal times, and sanitary conditions are among the matters dealt with. It is the function of local authorities to ensure that the law is complied with.

Weights and measures. Inspectors are appointed by local authorities to test weights and measures and to take proceedings against offenders.

(c) Necessary services

Public utilities. An important part of the activities of many local authorities is occupied with the provision of such public services as water supply, omnibuses, municipal markets, or other trading services. Local authorities are under no general compulsion to perform these services, but many have undertaken to do so in order to meet public demands and needs in the locality. In many places, these services are provided by private enterprise under statutory control.

Allotments and small holdings. Arrangements must (if there is sufficient local demand) be made by local authorities to provide land for allotments for vegetable growing, etc., and small holdings at suitable rents on assisted terms.

Burial and cremation. Cemeteries and crematoria are maintained by many local authorities.

Mortuaries may also be provided.

Remand homes for the accommodation of children and

young persons awaiting trial are provided by local authorities under the supervision of the Home Office.

(d) Records

Births, deaths, and marriages. Registration officers are appointed, and their offices are provided, by local authorities. The registers are kept at the local register office. The arrangements are under the central supervision of the Registrar General.

Electors. Registration of electors is performed by clerks of local councils as registration officers (see Chapter 3).

Land charges. To assist property owners and purchasers, a local land charges register must be kept showing local restrictions on land, e.g., town-planning restrictions, road charges, building requirements, and other limitations imposed on individual premises by local authorities. The registers must be open to inspection, and extracts supplied at a charge.

Motor vehicles and drivers' licences. The issue of licences for motor cars and drivers, and the collection of taxes and fees thereon are performed by county councils and county borough councils on behalf of the Central Government. Licences in respect of road haulage vehicles (carrier's licences) are issued by the chairman of the local Traffic Commissioners.

(VIII) GENERAL AND INCIDENTAL POWERS

Even the foregoing statement does not exhaust the list of powers possessed by local authorities. All local authorities have power to borrow money under certain conditions for the purpose of carrying out their duties (see Chapter 7). Land may be acquired by agreement or gift, or, with certain formalities, by compulsory purchase. By-laws may be made in respect of the property, services, and functions of local authorities, and also generally for the good rule and government of the locality. Further, local authorities may be assumed to have powers to do any act necessarily incidental to their other powers and duties, such as the purchase of stationery and printing, and the publication of information, etc.

General nature of local government. From all that has been said it will be seen that the variety and range of operations of local government authorities is considerable. It will also be appreciated that the word 'government' in its application to local authorities is justified in that the authorities have certain powers of control over citizens and their doings, but that local government involves largely the meeting of public needs by the provision of essential services.

Local authorities may, in a sense, be said to stand midway between Parliament and the people. The work of Parliament is mainly taken up with the making of laws. Parliament lays down enactments but takes little or no direct action to carry out its own laws. Local government authorities, however, besides having subordinate functions of a law-making character, as, for instance, the framing of by-laws and the imposition of requirements, have also a great deal to do in the enforcement and carrying out of laws, and in exercising functions of administration and management.

As a training for the citizen in the art of self-government, experience in the activities of local authorities can be very valuable. Many of our able parliamentarians and administrators have graduated to the larger realm of national affairs by way of a local council. A live interest in the work of one's local authority is a necessary expression of that informed and comprehending vigilance which is the honourable duty of every citizen in a free civilized society.

APPENDIX TO CHAPTER 4

The following lists are an attempt to show broadly the distribution of functions between the various classes of local authority. For the reasons stated in Chapter 4, the lists are not intended to be complete and exhaustive. They are, moreover, subject to considerable local variation.

—

COUNTY BOROUGH COUNCILS

Allotments, provision of

Baths, swimming baths, and wash-houses

Births, deaths, and marriages, registration

Blind, welfare of

Building, control of

By-laws, various

Cemeteries

Children, care, adoption, boarding out, control of employment

Civil defence

Common lodging houses, control of

Education, including school medical service and school meals

Electors, registration

Entertainments, provision of; licensing theatres, cinemas, racecourses

Fertilizers and feeding stuffs, analysis

Fire brigade

Food and drugs – milk and meat inspection, food sampling and analysis

Housing and slum clearance

Infectious disease, notification and disinfection

Land charges registration

Libraries and museums and art galleries

Local welfare service for aged and handicapped; accommodation and training

Local health services – maternity and child welfare, midwives, ambulance, health centres, home nursing

Mortuaries

Motor vehicles and drivers' licensing

Nuisances, suppression of

Nursing homes registration

Parks and open spaces

Petroleum storage and petrol stations

Police

Remand homes

Roads, streets, and bridges, maintenance and lighting

Sanitary services – drains, refuse collection and disposal, sewerage, smoke abatement

Shops inspection

Town planning

Vaccination

Weights and measures inspection

Wild birds protection

114

COUNTY COUNCILS

(Other than London)

Baths, swimming baths, and wash-houses

Births, deaths, and marriages, registration

Blind, welfare of

By-laws, various

Children, care, adoption, boarding out, control of employment

Civil defence

Education, including school medical service and school meals

Electors, registration

Entertainments, provision of; licensing theatres, cinemas, race-courses

Fertilizers and feeding stuffs analysis

Fire brigade

Food and drugs, inspection, sampling, and analysis

Housing (assistance in rural areas)

Infectious disease, notification and disinfection

Land charges registration

Libraries and museums and art galleries

Local welfare service for aged and handicapped, accommodation and training

Local health services – maternity and child welfare, midwives, ambulance, health centres, homes nursing

Motor vehicles and drivers' licensing

Nursing homes registration

Parks and open spaces

Police (*via* a Standing Joint Committee of the County Council and the County Justices)

Remand homes

Roads and bridges, construction and maintenance

Shops inspection

Town planning

Vaccination

Weights and measures inspection

Wild birds protection

NON-COUNTY BOROUGH COUNCILS

Allotments, provision of

Baths, swimming baths, and wash-houses

Building, control of

By-laws, various

Cemeteries

Common lodging houses, control of

Electors, registration

Entertainments, provision of

Food sampling, inspection of milk at shops and bottling establishments

Housing and slum clearance

Infectious diseases, notification and disinfection

Land charges registration

Libraries and museums and art galleries

Mortuaries

Nuisances, suppression of

Parks and open spaces

Petroleum storage and petrol stations

Roads, streets, and bridges

Sanitary services – drains, refuse collection and disposal, sewerage, smoke abatement

Shops inspection

Weights and measures inspection (if borough population over 10,000)

URBAN DISTRICT COUNCILS

Allotments, provision of

Baths, swimming baths, and wash-houses

Building, control of

By-laws, various

Cemeteries

Common lodging houses, control of

Electors, registration

Entertainments, provision of

Food sampling. Inspection of milk at shops and bottling establishments

Housing and slum clearance

Infectious diseases, notification and disinfection

Land charges registration

Libraries and museums and art galleries

Mortuaries

Nuisances, suppression of

Parks and open spaces

Petroleum storage and petrol stations

Roads and streets

Sanitary services – drains, refuse collection and disposal, sewerage, smoke abatement

Shops inspection (if population over 20,000)

RURAL DISTRICT COUNCILS

Baths, swimming baths, and wash-houses

By-laws, various

Building, control of

Cemeteries

Entertainments, provision of

Food sampling, milk inspection at shops and bottling establishments

Housing, and supervision of housing conditions

Infectious diseases, notification and disinfection

Land charges registration

Mortuaries

Nuisances, suppression of

Parks and open spaces

Sanitary services – sewerage, refuse collection and disposal, smoke abatement

Street lighting

PARISH COUNCILS

Allotments, provision of

Baths, swimming baths, and wash-houses

By-laws, various

Cemeteries

Footpaths (other than along roads), repair and maintenance

Housing (power to make representations to the county council)

Libraries

Mortuaries

Nuisances, suppression of

Parks and open spaces

Street lighting

LONDON COUNTY COUNCIL

Blind, welfare of

Building, control of

By-laws, various

Children, care, adoption, boarding out, control of employment

Education, including school medical service and school meals

Entertainments, provision of; licensing – theatres, cinemas, music and dancing, boxing

Fire brigade

Housing and slum clearance

Land charges registration

Local welfare service for aged and handicapped; accommodation and training

Local health services – maternity and child welfare, health centres, home nursing, ambulance, midwives

Motor vehicles and drivers' licensing

Museums and art galleries

Nursing homes registration

Parks and open spaces

Petroleum storage and petrol stations

Remand homes

Road construction, bridges (construction and maintenance)

Sewage disposal

Shops inspection

Street naming

Thames floods prevention

Town planning

Weights and measures inspection

METROPOLITAN BOROUGH COUNCILS

Allotments

Baths, swimming baths, and washhouses

Births, deaths, and marriages, registration

Bridges (minor)

By-laws, various

Cemeteries

Common lodging houses, control of

Drains and sewers (local)

Electors, registration

Food and drugs inspection

Housing

Land charges registration

Libraries, museums, and art galleries

Milk and dairies inspection

Mortuaries

Notification of disease, disinfection

Nuisances, suppression of

Parks and open spaces

Refuse removal and disposal

Street lighting, cleansing, and maintenance

Street markets

CITY OF LONDON CORPORATION

Births, deaths, and marriages, registration

Bridges

By-laws, various

Cemeteries

Common lodging houses, control of

Food and drugs inspection

117

CITY OF LONDON CORPORATION – *continued*

Housing
Land charges registration
Libraries, museums, and art galleries
Markets, main and street
Milk and dairies inspection
Mortuaries
Notification of disease and disinfection
Nuisances, suppression of

Parks and open spaces
Petroleum storage and petrol stations
Police
Port health authority
Refuse removal and disposal
Shops inspection
Street lighting, cleaning, and maintenance
Weights and measures inspection

CHAPTER 5

HOW THEY DO IT

THE work which a local authority has to do is of a very mixed character and embraces functions of a varied kind. In a small area, where the population runs into a few thousands only, and the council consists of no more than 20 or 30 members, it would be quite possible for all the business of the local authority to be done by the council itself at a few meetings a year. Any matters of minor importance that arose between meetings could be dealt with by the officers of the council, after consultation if need be with the chairman or other leading members, and, if something specially important arose, a special meeting of the council could be summoned to deal with it.

But the council of a very large area could not carry on efficiently in this way. Local government affairs are, especially in the case of counties and large towns, rather complex; indeed municipal work gets more complex year by year as public services develop and more and more duties are given by Parliament to local authorities.

Appointment of committees. Most local authorities therefore make use of the opportunity which the law gives to all of them to appoint committees. It seems to be a universal rule in human affairs that the fewer the number of persons who have to deal with a job, the quicker that job gets done. A committee of a dozen or twenty, or, if the work to be done requires it, thirty members, is more likely to get hold of a job and make some shape of it than a council of a hundred members. Parliament has recognized this by itself appointing its own committees. Bills introduced into Parliament go, after approval at first and second reading, to a committee which, after discussing it, and amending it as need be, reports it back to the whole House for further consideration.

The committees of local authorities work much after the same fashion. Business which is initiated in the full council, as when a proposal is moved, seconded, and agreed to, that a certain subject shall be considered, is, where the council has committees, almost invariably referred to a committee for consideration and report, before the council comes to a final decision.

The committee system of local authorities has one great difference from that of Parliament. In Parliament almost all of the business has to come before the full House first, before it can go to a committee. But the general practice among local authorities is for certain branches of the council's business to be delegated to its several committees. As a result of this practice, the bulk of the business of a local authority which has appointed committees goes to the committees first, who may be empowered, within certain limits, to deal with the business entirely themselves. Items of major importance or of principle are reserved for the full council to deal with. Such items, after having gone to the appropriate committee, are made the subject of reports by the committee to the council with such recommendations for action as the committee may have decided on. The council thus gets the advantage of the advice of its committees, and can decide to accept or not the advice offered.

The advantages of having committees. The objects attained by appointing committees are several. First the council's business is divided up among the members. Instead of every member having to concern himself with every piece of business which comes to the local authority, a member need only concern himself with the business which comes before the committees of which he happens to be a member, and, of course, with such items of business as come before the full council. Secondly, the council, by delegating much work to committees for them to deal with entirely, is able to get through its business more quickly. Thirdly, and most important of all, the council, by making a practice of referring everything first to a committee, and instructing that committee to report thereon to the council, gets the advantage of having that business done in two stages. In other words the council, by referring an item to a committee for consideration and report, gives itself the chance of thinking twice.

In Parliament, and in the national governmental assemblies of most countries, there are two Houses or chambers. The general rule is that proposals approved by one House cannot become law until those proposals have also been approved by the other House. This system has been adopted throughout the civilized world because it gives an opportunity for two sets of minds to contribute thought to the business of government. But in the constitution of local government authorities this 'second house' principle does not apply; the council sits as one assembly. Although the body of aldermen are elected in a different fashion from the councillors, and for a different period, and may therefore be considered as a sort of senate or local peerage, they do not sit apart from the councillors, or form a separate chamber. The equivalent of the second-house principle is, in local government, the committee system.

For the most part the local authority has a very wide discretion as to whether it will appoint committees, what committees it will appoint, the degree to which it will authorize its committees to perform the authority's work, the degree to which the council will exercise control over its committees, the personnel of committees, and the frequency of their meetings. Parliament has, however, to some extent, limited this discretion.

Statutory committees. Doubtless recognizing the value of the committee method of dealing with local affairs, Parliament has laid it down that for certain functions some local authorities must appoint committees. Local authorities which have education functions or functions in relation to the care of children must appoint an education committee or a children's committee respectively; in boroughs which have a separate police force of their own, the borough council must appoint a committee for that purpose known by the antique name of the Watch Committee. Such committees are commonly known as 'statutory committees'.

Control of committees. The degree of control retained by the council over its committees varies with circumstances. The extreme example is that of the Watch Committee of a borough council. Although by law the decisions of that committee need no confirmation by the borough council, indeed, cannot be overruled by the council, none the less it is the council who appoints the members of the Watch Committee, and it is the council who finds the money for the committee to spend.* In this way the council has some degree of ultimate control over the committee.

The general rule with regard to other committees is that all

*The position with regard to county police is somewhat similar although, as indicated in chapter 2, the county police authority is a Standing Joint Committee of the county council and the justices. The county council appoints its own representatives and finds the money for the Joint Committee to spend, but it has no other control over the Joint Committee.

their acts are subject to approval by the council and that no committee can raise a rate or borrow money. In this way committees are continuously subject to such control and supervision as the council may wish to exercise over them. The degree of control and supervision is a matter for the council itself to settle.

Personnel of committees. Except in the case of a Watch Committee, the members of a committee need not all be members of the council which appoints the committee. Normally two thirds of the members of a committee must be members of the council; but an Education Committee and a Children's Committee need only include a majority of members of the appointing council.

These opportunities of appointing (or co-opting) to committees persons who are not members of the council enables a council to enlist the services of men and women who are interested in the work of the committees and have special experience. Indeed, the law requires that an Education Committee and a Children's Committee must have some members specially qualified or experienced in the subjects dealt with by those committees respectively.

The qualifications and disqualifications applicable to members of a council (see Chapter 3) apply generally also to members of committees. Committees usually appoint their own chairmen and vice-chairmen, although sometimes these are appointed by the council itself.

Standing and special committees. The number of committees which a local authority appoints depends, of course, on the amount and type of work which that authority has to do. Where its work includes matters for which a statutory committee must be appointed the authority has no choice but to appoint a committee. But the requirements of the Acts of Parliament which make the appointment of statutory committees obligatory do not necessarily preclude the local authority from giving to a statutory committee work other than that which the Acts require to be given to the committee.

Subject to these considerations, the local authority decides, usually at its statutory annual meeting, what committees it will appoint, and who shall be the members of those committees. The committees which are appointed regularly year by year to carry out work which is part of the normal functions are 'standing committees'. Besides these, the authority may, from time to time, decide to appoint 'special committees' to deal with some unusual piece of work of a temporary character.

Examples of standing committees appointed by a county borough council are: Finance Committee (for general financial control); Highways Committee (to deal with street works and maintenance); Housing Committee (to build and manage council houses); Town Planning Committee (to make and administer town planning schemes); Public Health Committee (to see to sewerage, food and drugs sampling, infectious diseases, and the provision of clinics); the Water Committee (if the Council runs a water supply undertaking); a Cemeteries Committee (to provide and manage cemeteries). Other standing committees, whose functions are obvious from the names of the committees, are the Parks Committee, the Libraries Committee, and the Markets Committee.

If the number of theatres and cinemas in the area of the authority is large, it will be convenient to have a Theatres or Entertainments Committee. Some authorities have a committee to manage their staff, or to deal with all the purchases of goods, or to exercise the various functions of control in relation to shops, petrol stations, explosives, weights and measures, employment agencies, and motor-car licensing.

Instances of special committees are: Unemployment Committee (appointed during a slump to provide work for local unemployed), or an Evacuation Committee (to deal with the evacuation of children from danger zones in wartime). The emergence into special prominence of a particular local question requiring investigation, arrangements for special ceremonies (as during the coronation period), or some unusual and heavy litigation involving special action, may each make it desirable for the authority to appoint a special committee. There is no difference between the functioning of standing and special committees; the only general difference is that special committees go out of existence when the particular work for which they were appointed is accomplished.

It is the almost invariable rule for every local authority which appoints committees to have a General Purposes Committee. This committee deals with matters not specially referred to other committees, and, in general practice ranks as the premier committee. Frequently the chairmen of the other committees are members of it, and it forms a kind of Cabinet of the local authority. It will settle matters of general policy, and perhaps arrange differences between other committees. Broad issues affecting the work of the local authority as a whole will be considered by it. The internal organization of the authority, the structure of its departments, and the distribution of the work among committees are matters on which it is usual for the General Purposes Committee to advise the council.

Sub-committees. In the case of a very large local authority the total work to be distributed among committees is itself so huge that each committee's share is more than it can manage by ordinary committee meetings. In such cases it is the practice for the committee to appoint sub-committees. The Education Committee for a large county or county borough may have as many as six or more sub-committees to deal each with a particular sub-division of the education work. Appointments of teaching staff, the selection and provision of books and apparatus, the erection and maintenance of school buildings, the settlement of curricula, the award of scholarships, primary, secondary, and technical education, and evening schools, for instance, are all matters on which separate sub-committees can be appointed. Where the authority has a large area for the administration of local health services, local sub-committees of the Health Committee are appointed to administer local arrangements. It is usual to appoint a managing sub-committee for each school or other institution owned and run by the local authority.

In this way the number of sub-committees can be, in the case of a large authority, very numerous. There will be not only sub-committees of main committees but local managing sub-committees for institutions, schools and homes, and possibly area sub-committees for housing and health services. The total of all these may run into hundreds. The work of some of these sub-committees may be substantial enough to justify the appointment of 'sections' or sub-committees of the sub-committees to deal, subject to general principles laid down for the guidance of the sections, with such matters as the interviewing of applicants for minor appointments, the grant of licences for building work of a routine character, or similar matters not involving major principles.

Committees and departments. The internal organization of a local authority with the average range of functions is that of a multi-sided business with several departments. In a typical county borough there will be the council itself, with its group of committees, and sub-committees, sharing the work of the council. Behind this range of assemblies is the departmental structure. There will be a finance department to collect the income of the council and to pay its expenses. There will be other departments such as the medical or health department, the parks department, the surveyor's or engineer's department, and so on. These departments may coincide with the various committees of the council. The finance department, for example, serves the Finance Committee; the public health department may act as the departmental counterpart to the Public Health Committee. Perfect accord between committee structure and departmental structure is not, of course, necessary, nor is it always possible to arrange it.

Procedure – Standing orders. Over all this organization, both of committees and departments, the council is the master. Ultimately all power and responsibility is with the council. Not only are the work of each committee, and their membership and frequency of meeting defined by the council, but the manner in which they shall carry out their duties is laid down. The mode of voting, their obligations to report their doings to the council, the amount of money they shall spend, and the minimum number of members (quorum) who can properly transact the business of a committee are prescribed. Further, the duties of the principal officers, their duties towards the committees, and the powers of the committees over the officers are also defined. Such matters as these are laid down in the council's standing orders.

Each local authority has its own set of standing orders, the number and complexity of which depend on the size of the council's organization. The standing orders also lay down the procedure to be followed in relation to meetings of the council, the conduct of debate, length of speeches, and the method of dealing with motions and amendments. The form in which the decisions of the council and committees shall be recorded in the minutes of each meeting, the procedure to be followed in approving expenditure, making contracts and accepting tenders, and the general conditions of appointment of staff are also subjects commonly dealt with in standing orders.

In some few matters Parliament has prescribed how the business of a council itself shall be transacted. The mode of election of aldermen is an example, referred to in Chapter 3. The Third Schedule to the Local Government Act, 1933 (in the case of London the London Government Act, 1939), lays down rules as to the annual and quarterly and other meetings of councils, the mode of convening meetings, the quorum, and the mode of voting. Minutes must be kept and signed. But every council may, and generally does, make supplementary standing orders to elaborate (although not to contravene) the provisions which Parliament has made in these respects. Many councils meet more often than the four times a year required by law. Monthly meetings are a common practice, while busy authorities may meet fortnightly or even weekly.

Copies of the standing orders of a local council are generally available for reference at the local public library, and may be purchasable. In 1950, the Ministry of Housing and Local Government issued a model series of standing orders for the guidance of local authorities; copies of these were placed on sale by H.M. Stationery Office.

Devolution of responsibility. Comparison with commercial practice. After this brief review of the internal organization of a local government authority it is possible to appreciate the one great difference between that organization and the organization of a normal commercial company. In a public company there are three sets of persons involved in the carrying on of the business – the owners of the business (the shareholders), the board of directors, who settle general policy, and the servants and officers of the company.

If you like to compare the body of shareholders with the body of electors in a local governmental area, the comparison will be defensible. The shareholders appoint the policy-making body, i.e., the board of directors; and the local government electors elect the local council. After that, the opportunities which both shareholders and electors have of making their influence felt upon the body they have appointed or elected are few and indirect.

In the internal working of a local authority there is, however, as will have been seen, a body of committees which forms a layer between the policy-making council and the servants or officers. In a commercial concern much is left to be done by individual members of the staff, the sales manager, the advertising manager, the works manager, and the managing director. These have their several duties and responsibilities, and, if need be, can get together and form small committees among themselves to discuss how best to carry on the firm's work. They are answerable to and receive their instruction from the board of directors. There is, in normal practice, no committee system comparable with that of the local government world.

The reason for this difference is twofold. First, local authorities are unable for the most part, and unwilling, to pass on their responsibilities to officers or servants. Local authorities do, of course, have to leave much to their officers; but the fact remains that the law in general requires that the acts of a local authority shall be performed or authorized by a council itself or by a committee appointed by it. Local authorities are responsible to the local public at large, and not merely to a section of the public such as forms the body of shareholders of a company – a very limited section after all, however large the company may be. Accordingly, the members of local councils are hesitant at letting too much get into the hands of the officers of the council. The council cannot avoid responsibility for the services provided by it. While local government remains what it is in this country, there can be no wholesale devolution of responsibility to individual officers as there is in the organization of a commercial concern.

In some countries of the world, as was indicated in Chapter 1, the practice has been adopted of allowing much of the normal work of local government to be carried on by city managers, subject to broad supervision by the elected council. This practice, which, where adopted, brings local government into closer comparability with commercial organization, reduces democratic control to a minimum. It is, for that reason, open to question whether it will ever be widely adopted in this country.

The absence of the profit motive. The second reason why the committee system of local authorities has no counterpart in commercial practice is that in the world of commerce the standard of efficiency is measurable by cost and profit. A successful managing director or departmental manager is one who produces the greatest profit for the firm. When deciding whether to embark on a new venture, take up the manufacture or sale of new commodities, or provide a new service, the commercial man has only one big question to ask, 'Will it pay?' Local authorities cannot ask themselves that question – at least in only a very few cases. An authority that runs a transport or water-supply undertaking, can ask itself, 'Does it pay?' and the answer will, in the broad sense, be the measure of the efficiency of the undertaking.

Accordingly, it is possible to delegate the running of such undertakings almost entirely to officers, to a manager, or engineer. If the public gets efficient service at the right price, that is, in general, all there is to it; the local authority can leave the job to its officers, and retain, like a board of directors, general control and the formation of policy.

But when it comes to the other services to be provided by a local authority the question of profit cannot and ought not to arise. Should for instance the running of a maternity and child welfare service show a profit? The question has only to be asked to show how absurd it is. In the case of services such as primary and secondary education, road maintenance, and domestic refuse collection – services in respect of which the actual recipient has, as such, no fees to pay – the operation of the services cannot be run on a profit and loss basis. Even where fees are charged, as for the use of swimming baths, libraries, and games pitches in parks, the fees must always be scaled down so as not to produce an unduly large income. A local authority whose general income level became substantially higher than its expenditure would soon find itself unpopular. The ratepayers would at once demand that the rates should be lowered, so that income met expenditure, and no more. Broadly speaking, local government, like national government, must not show a profit – financially, that is.

In the case of such services as maternity and child welfare the question of financial profit cannot arise at all. Although extravagance should be avoided, the question of how much benefit is obtained for so much cost cannot be mathematically ascertained. The benefits of such a service are imponderable, and can be measured only in terms of health, happiness, or general welfare of mother and child. Doubtless these things do, in turn, have an effect on national efficiency. It is beyond question that a service of this kind ought to yield, in the national sense, an indirect profit by providing a saving in the nation's expenditure on other health services. But however you may look at it, the fact remains that the local authority in this and most other services cannot use the profit standard as the measure of efficiency. The lack of such a standard makes it impolitic to delegate entirely to officers the running of all local services. The members of the local authority must do a substantial part of the work themselves.

And in doing that work, they must bring to it qualities of judgement and experience which take into account complex factors which include the local needs, local taste and demand, political feeling, local rate-paying capacity, efficiency of the service, the requirements of Parliament, and the trends of social development. The business man has (it is true) to do this in relation to his business, but he has the advantage of being able to watch his profit and loss account and see from it whether he is succeeding or not. The member of a local authority can tell whether he is a success or not only by submitting, at the end of his three years' term of office, to a local public election. And even if he fails at the election, that does not necessarily prove him to be wrong; for the electorate is fickle, and all sorts of considerations affect the election result. The member of a local government authority must, if he wishes to go on being a member, watch his step all the time.

The tempo of local government. For all these reasons, and because local authorities have to do their work against the continuous strong light of public opinion, the methods of dealing with business appear to be slow in comparison with those of the commercial world. A person who writes a letter to his local council may get an answer in a day or two. This is unlikely. A delay of a week or two is more

132

likcly. It may be a matter of a month or two before he gets (apart from a bare acknowledgement of his letter) a substantial answer.

The reason for this is that, if the inquiry is on a small point, the answer can be given by an official without having to consult anyone else – the point may be one on which the official has been authorized to act. If the matter is more substantial, it will have to go before a committee, before a reply can be sent. Committees may meet weekly, in the case of a busy local authority, or they may meet fortnightly or monthly, or even more seldom. Accordingly the reply has to wait until the committee have met; but that is not quite all. The committee themselves are not likely to deal with the matter at first hand; they will ask the advice of their officers. If the point is difficult, the officer will take a few days to consider his advice. He may think it necessary to consult with his fellow officers. In this way, the matter may not be ripe for the next meeting of the appropriate committee – it may have to wait for the meeting after next – a week or a month hence.

If the point is very important indeed, it may be outside the competence of a committee, and may have to go to the full council. The council may meet quarterly, or more frequently, according to the local authority. The committee which has dealt with the matter will submit a report to the council indicating what action the committee recommends should be taken by the council. These committee reports are usually printed in the agenda paper for the council meeting. After the council has arrived at its decision, the appropriate reply is sent to the inquirer, who, by that time, may have waited several weeks for it.

It is a common practice among local authorities to arrange for the chairman of the council or of a committee to act on behalf of the council or a committee between meetings. Although this helps to bridge the gap, it does not save delay in every case; for there are some matters which the chairman will not deal with in this way, either because his authority is limited, or because he prefers, on account of the difficulty or importance of the matter, to let it wait for the next meeting.

All this is part of the price paid for democratic local government. If the official who received the letter in the first place had not had to put the matter to a committee, who in turn had to put the matter to the full council, the official could have dealt with the matter in perhaps a few days.

General mode of conducting business. From all this can be gained a hint of what goes on at an ordinary meeting of a council or a committee. Business may arise in two ways, by being put before the meeting by an official, or by being brought up by members. It is the general duty of the officers of a local authority to bring before the appropriate meeting everything which ought to be dealt with at that meeting. The clerk of a local council is in the position of a secretary; his function is to conduct the principal correspondence of the council, and to record and communicate the decisions of the council and of the committees. He and the other officials, whoever they may be, medical officer, engineer, or treasurer, are under an obligation to keep the council and its committees informed on what is going on in the various departments of the authority's work. They are also required to advise the committees on matters arising before the committees.

Committee meetings. When a meeting of a committee is required, the clerk of the authority will send out a notice calling the members together. He will also send out an agenda paper showing what business is due to be transacted at the meeting. The agenda will consist (among other items) of letters received and which require an answer, and reports by officers asking for permission to make purchases of equipment, or to employ staff, or to carry out certain operations, e.g., the mending of a road or the repair of one of the council's buildings. The officers may also have to submit reports monthly or quarterly of the state of the work of their departments, with any other information of interest to the committee. There may also be, on the agenda paper, matters which have, by resolution of the council, been referred to the committee for consideration and report. Lastly, there may be proposals to be discussed by the committee at the instance of a member who has given notice to have the matters discussed.

The agenda paper will show all this, either set out in full or in summarized form. Very often, reports and other statements of information, copies of letters, and other documents to be considered are not set out in full on the agenda paper, but are sent out separately with it. All these papers are sent out two days or more before the committee meets, so that the members may have time to study them, and be the more able to discuss them when the meeting takes place. It is easy to appreciate that the member of a busy local authority may have quite a lot to do, especially if he or she is a member of more than one committee. It is not unusual for the papers for a meeting of an important committee of a busy local authority to run into fifty or more typewritten or printed sheets, some of them interesting, some of them dull statistics or dry formal information. Some of the matters may be complex and really difficult, demanding close study and a great deal of thought. All this is done by members of local authorities who are, unpaid, and yet are often subject to much public criticism. The job of being a member of a busy local authority is no sinecure.

Committee decisions. As the committee comes to its decisions on the various matters on the agenda paper, the decisions are duly recorded by the clerk. Action then follows after the meeting according to circumstances. If a reply has to be sent, and the matter is within the competence of the committee, the clerk sends the reply in the name of the authority. If stores have to be bought or work done, the appropriate officer will receive from the clerk a copy of the committee's decision or some indication in some other form that the purchase or work has been authorized by the committee and can be performed. If the matter is one for the council itself, the clerk and his assistants will set about drafting a report to be submitted by the committee to the council.

Council meeting – Admission of the public. The convening of meetings of the council and the conduct of business there is done in much the same way as for meetings of committees. The council meetings are rather more formal affairs; members usually stand up to speak, which they do not in committee, and usually a member can speak only once on each item of business, whereas in a committee a member may speak on each item as often as he can get the chance. Meetings of the council must be open to the public. There is usually a public gallery.

This right of admission extends also to representatives of the press. The press and public must also be admitted to meetings of committees composed of all the members of a local authority, to meetings of an education committee and of any joint committee or joint board of local authorities. If at any time a council, board, or committee consider that any item of business should, in the public interest, not be discussed in public, the press can be excluded during the discussion of that item. The press have no statutory right to attend other committees or sub-committees; but there is nothing to prevent a local authority, if it so wishes, from granting admission to such meetings. Indeed, some local authorities make a regular practice of it. Admission in such cases is a concession which can be withdrawn if the press do not show fairness and proper discretion in their reports.

The presence of the public and the press has its effect on the demeanour of members and on the conduct of the business. Speeches are more carefully phrased, both with an eye to publicity, and with regard to the possibility that what is uttered in public may later give the speaker occasion for regret, or be held up against him.

The agenda paper for a council meeting consists almost entirely of reports by committees of the council, either informing the council of the state of work under the committees' charge, or recommending that the council should take certain action or express certain opinions. Notices of motion may also be set down for discussion by members of the council. If any urgent or unforeseen situation arises, it is generally competent, according to the standing orders of the council, for a member to propose 'That the council do now adjourn'. Such a motion for adjournment is often resorted to in order to provide the occasion for making speeches of protest or to draw attention to something special. If the motion succeeds, then the council meeting is adjourned to the next ordinary day of meeting.

Voting at meetings of the council is by show of hands. If, however, a certain number of members demand it, a 'division' is taken. This means that the way each member votes is put down in writing. The clerk may read out the names of the members one by one, giving each member the opportunity to say out loud which way he votes 'For' or 'Against' or 'Not voting'. An alternative method is that followed in Parliament, where all the members go through one door if they wish to vote 'For', or through another door if they wish to vote 'Against'. As the members pass through the appropriate door, their names are marked off on a list.

The practice of voting by means of a division is used when it is desired to make each member face up to responsibility. When voting is taken by show of hands, the chairman or the clerk counts the hands held up, and may or may not give an indication of the numbers voting each way. The announcement is made that the motion is lost, or is carried as the case may be; and no indication whatever is given as to which way each individual member voted. The taking of votes on a division, however, indicates which way each member votes, besides being a more accurate way of counting the number of votes.

The practice of requiring a division to be taken is frequently adopted where political feelings enter into local affairs. The name of every member voting on a division and the way in which he voted is set out in full in the minutes of the council. Minutes of a council have to be printed, and are open to inspection by any local government elector on payment of a fee not exceeding one shilling, and the elector may make a copy of any part of the minutes. Most local authorities, in view of this, publish their minutes and place them on sale.

As a result, the way in which members vote on a division becomes or can become public property. The taking of a division serves therefore to register publicly, as regards the subject voted on, the views of the parties on the council, and also enables the political organizers to check the party loyalty of the members.

Politics in local government. In spite of widespread opinion that politics should not enter into local government affairs, it is a fact that, in many local authorities, there exist well-organized party divisions. Elections are frequently run on party lines, and the usual party discipline is applied to the members by their political organizations. The London County Council, from its inception in 1889, has had clearly defined party divisions between its members. In the big industrial areas of the country the local government authorities are frequently organized on political party lines. In the rural areas and among county councils generally, political organization for local government purposes hardly exists at all.

Although it is undoubtedly justifiable to argue that the aim of democratic government should be to attract into public affairs the best men and women irrespective of party considerations, and although it is quite true that many of the matters dealt with by local authorities are of the nature of a business undertaking in which political opinions are not relevant, the fact remains that, where public money is being spent on services, it is very likely that opinions about how best to run those services will be sharply divided between those who, on the one hand, take the view that the emphasis should lie chiefly towards the public benefits to be provided, and those on the other hand whose view is that the main emphasis should be directed towards the ratepayer whose pockets suffer in any case. There are, of course, other possible lines of division, and many degrees of opinion within those divisions; but, in practice, the differences do in the main accord with the broad division between the socialist who urges greater municipalization and the extension of free services for all, and the non-socialist whose views tend towards a more individualistic attitude.

Political organization in local government affairs does have the undoubted advantage, as it does in Parliament, of bringing greater coherence and definition into the policy of the governing body. Where the parties are well organized and disciplined, it is possible to get a decision more quickly than when there is no such organization. This is particularly the case in the period between meetings. The leader of the majority party on a council can (like a Prime Minister) speak with authority on behalf of his administration and virtually bind it in advance.

In local government affairs there are often important matters which, before being put to a council or a committee for decision, require discussion and negotiation. Wage agreements, schemes for the carrying out of works involving the purchase of land, arrangements for the sharing of services between two authorities are examples of the kind of subject which may need considerable private discussion between the interests concerned before the matter can be put into a suitable shape for submission to the council or a committee. If, in the course of those discussions, there is someone representing the local authority who can speak with some sureness, and with foreknowledge of what the local authority is likely to approve, the discussions are easier to conduct. The leader of a political group in power or a representative who can speak with authority on behalf of that group, can be much more sure of his touch when conducting such discussions, and those with whom he is discussing can feel that what he says is more likely to be adopted by the council than when discussions are conducted by a representative who has no such backing.

This is not to say that the introduction of politics in local government does not have disadvantages similar to those which it is alleged to have in parliamentary affairs. Party discipline necessarily limits the freedom of members, the real power tends to drift into the hands of the few leading politicians, and there is the possibility that the party organization, instead of the elected council, may become the real governing body. To all this there is one stock answer – that no matter how well devised the organization of government may be, if the machine is run by bad people, the government will be bad; but, if the government is run by honest clear-thinking industrious people who have the good of the public at heart, then the government will be good in spite of defects in the organization. Politicians know this as well as anybody. You can't fool all the people all of the time. Administration must be sound if it is to endure. Local politicians, like all other politicians, passionately want to endure. Their administration must be able to stand up to public criticism, and be fair, be sensitive to public needs, and be incorrupt.

Disability on account of pecuniary interest. These reflexions prompt the mention of another topic which is frequently the subject of misunderstanding among the public in general. Many persons are quite convinced that members of local authorities get elected for personal and private reasons, that they get something out of their membership – meaning of course that, directly or indirectly, there are monetary advantages, opportunities for improving one's business connexions, or some other financial gain to be got by becoming a member of a local council.

There is a very grave misconception in all this. To start with, the law provides that if any member of a local authority has any pecuniary interest, direct or indirect (whether by himself or through his partner, or wife, or through any company of which he is a member of nominee), in any contract or proposed contract, or other matter which is being considered or dealt with by the local authority, the member shall, if he is present at any meeting of the council or of a committee where the matter in question is being discussed, disclose his interest, be prohibited from taking part in the discussion and must not vote on any question arising out of the matter. Failure to comply with these provisions constitutes a criminal offence and involves penalties.

None the less, scandals, or the suspicion of scandals, in local government affairs do at times arise, in spite of the legal requirements. But scandals are really quite few and very limited in scope. The fact that a great fuss is made when any misdoing on the part of a councillor or alderman is suspected demonstrates at once that the greatest safeguard against corruption in office is a live and active public opinion.

There is, of course, a certain type of elector who thinks that, because he once voted for a candidate, this gives him a right to ask the candidate (when he becomes a member) to use influence on the elector's behalf. It is sometimes difficult for a member to resist requests of this kind. There is a general feeling that a member exists to serve the interests of the electors, and it is not always easy to determine whether a member, in doing a good turn for an elector, is serving public or private interests. The cardinal fact remains, however, that public opinion does not countenance misdoings in public office. Public representatives and political parties are very anxious to look well in the eyes of the public. There is always someone ready to find fault. In a small local authority it is not easy to keep a secret for very long; in a small town everybody's business is, more or less, everybody else's business. In the case of a large local authority the machine is too big to be tampered with – there are too many people concerned in the administration to make opportunities for wrong-doing.

It is, of course, true that, by getting on to a local council, you run into all sorts of local personalities and people of influence. You may get a social thrill out of that. But you won't find those people wanting to put private business in your way just because you happen to be a member of the council. You will be respected only according to what you put into your public work, not by what you seek to get out of it.

Members' expenses. Members of local authorities and of committees are by law entitled to claim their travelling expenses incurred in carrying out approved official duties such as attending meetings and performing inspections, but not normally in attending ceremonies. They can also claim subsistence allowances and allowances for loss of earnings and expense incurred in performing their official work.

All these payments are quite small, are strictly limited, are subject to maxima prescribed by Act of Parliament or by the Minister of Housing and Local Government, are a reimbursement of expense actually and necessarily incurred and are not of the nature of a salary or remuneration. A register, open to public inspection, must be kept of the amounts paid to each member. Some members make no claim at all.

The member's contribution to public work. The very great majority of persons serving on local councils do so without thought of material rewards. The urge is mainly psychological. Idealism to a certain extent plays a part. The promptings of self-expression may, in one form or another, provide a motive. But, after all, there is nothing necessarily blameworthy in that. It is a natural instinct to seek occupation that fits one's talents. It is, to those people who are that way inclined, a satisfying thing to be in the swim of public affairs, to be able to take the chair at a meeting, to employ the title of alderman or councillor, to make public speeches and come out at the top of the poll. That, and the great sense of doing work that is worth while, is about all there is to it.

Once the genuine interest in public work takes hold of a man or a woman, it seems very difficult to resist. Other ulterior and sinister motives are extremely rare. Even the much talked of 'will to power' – the desire to order other people about – plays a very small part (if any) in prompting a person to take up the burden of public duties.

The extent of this willing and unpaid burden is not sufficiently appreciated by the public. Any person who thinks only of making money should not get himself elected to a local authority. For such a person the obvious course is surely to go and devote his energies to his own private concerns, and not to take up time sitting on a local council or committee. The members of a council, that is those who count, use up a great deal of their private time on council affairs. The principal members of a busy local authority may easily spend half their waking hours on council matters – meetings, discussions, visits to institutions, ceremonies, and the like. And most of it demands heavy brain work. Doubtless they enjoy it, but they certainly do not get rich over it. As for the back-bencher, if he spends rather less time on public affairs, his opportunities of getting anything out of it are correspondingly less.

Democracy is under a great obligation to the public representative both in national and local affairs. Indeed, local democratic government on the British model cannot function at all without the great voluntary efforts of thousands of publicly elected representatives on local government authorities up and down the country. They may get a kick out of it (sometimes a few kicks from behind); they may get pride and satisfaction out of their public work; but they get little else. The public owes to its elected representatives an immeasurable debt which is too little and too seldom recognized.

CHAPTER 6

LOCAL GOVERNMENT OFFICIALS

EVERY local authority has powers to appoint its own officials, and to pay them. The extent of these powers depends on the status of the local authority. A parish council may appoint only two officers, a clerk and a treasurer. These may be members of the parish council, or may be appointed from outside the council. The clerk may be paid, but only if he is not a member of the parish council. The parish treasurer never gets any pay.

Compulsory appointments. All local authorities are required by law to appoint a clerk. He is known as the town clerk in the case of a borough, and as the clerk of the council in the case of other authorities. The council is required by law to pay him a reasonable salary.

With regard to other appointments, the local authority is somewhat in the same position as it is in regard to the appointment of committees. There are some appointments which must be made. These obligatory appointments depend on the functions which the local authority has to perform. Every county council must appoint a county medical officer of health (who by law must be a qualified medical practitioner with a diploma in public health or its equivalent), a county surveyor, and a county treasurer. A borough council (whether county, non-county, or metropolitan) is obliged by law to appoint a medical officer of health, a surveyor, a public health inspector, and a treasurer. An urban or rural district council must also have a medical officer of health, sanitary inspector, surveyor, and treasurer. Boroughs

146

outside London may also have to appoint auditors (see Chapter 7).

In addition to all these, there are certain other appointments which a council is required to make in order to carry out duties which have been imposed by law upon the council. For instance, an authority carrying out duties in relation to the care of children deprived of a normal home life must appoint a special and suitably qualified children's officer. A chief education officer with proper qualifications and experience must be appointed by every local education authority, together with an appropriate staff of qualified teachers and instructors. An authority responsible for the local fire brigade must maintain the brigade at proper strength.

Public analysts, shops inspectors, inspectors of weights and measures, chief constables, coroners, registrars of births, deaths, and marriages, registration officers for election purposes, must, by various Acts of Parliament, be appointed by the authorities concerned in the administration of those Acts. All these compulsory appointments may be paid.

In making some of these compulsory appointments the local authority are, to a certain extent, under the control of a central Department of Government. For instance, the salary paid to the clerk of a county council outside London must be approved by the Minister of Housing and Local Government, and the clerk cannot be dismissed except with the Minister's consent. A chief education officer or a children's officer may not be appointed unless the appropriate Minister is satisfied that the appointee is suitable. Sometimes, the Government Department has power to prescribe the qualifications which persons must have before being appointed; for instance, medical officers of boroughs and county districts, health visitors, and public health inspectors must have such qualifications as the Minister of Health requires, and inspectors of weights and measures must be certified by the Board of Trade as having the proper qualifications for the work.

In some cases the official cannot be appointed or dismissed without the approval of the Government Department. Thus public analysts and certain senior whole-time public health inspectors may be appointed or dismissed only with the approval of the Minister of Health in each case. The dismissal of a medical officer of health requires similar approval. But apart from such special cases as these (and they are comparatively few) a local authority has complete independence as to whom it shall appoint to a particular job, and what salary shall be paid.

Local authorities may appoint deputies of the holders of the compulsory appointments.

Discretionary appointments. In addition, a local authority, other than a parish council, has a general power to appoint such staff as it needs, and to pay such remuneration as the council thinks fit. The staff usually appointed depends, here again, on the functions which the council has to carry out.

The range of such appointments is very wide and includes staff with high professional, technical, and managerial qualifications and experience, down to clerical staff, porters, messengers, and workpeople. The higher grades of staff are usually called 'officers', because they hold an 'office' or official position; the lesser grades are termed 'servants'.

The discretionary appointments commonly made include the following: librarians, inspectors of food and drugs, nurses, a solicitor, an architect, land agent, housing manager, catering manager, town-planning officer, water engineers (where the council runs a water service), an entertainments manager or publicity officer. In addition, there may be a body of road-sweepers, dustmen, cemetery and swimming-bath attendants, park-keepers, and the like.

Conditions of service. Apart from the special cases where appointment or dismissal requires the approval of a Government Department, the staff are all appointed at the pleasure of the Council and, unless there are any special terms agreed as to notice of dismissal, an officer or servant of a local authority can be dismissed on the spot without notice and without any reason. This is, however, very seldom done. The tendency of all local authorities is to make appointments for all practical purposes on a permanent basis.

Some staff may be engaged on a weekly or monthly basis. 'Temporary' appointments of this kind are usual in the case of workpeople, minor clerical staff, and in the case of special jobs created for an unusual, e.g. wartime, purpose. Where a local authority has to enter on a great slum-clearance scheme, or an enlarged educational programme requiring the erection of many new schools, or where an unusually heavy amount of housing work, or of road improvement schemes has to be undertaken, it is a frequent practice of local authorities to employ staff on a non-permanent basis for so long as the unusual amount of work exists. Local authorities may also appoint persons for a special piece of work, e.g., a town planning consultant to make a town-planning scheme, a medical specialist to advise on a certain problem, or an architect to design a new town hall or other public building.

In general, however, a person who obtains employment on the staff of a local council can, with good behaviour, count on being employed permanently.

Salaries. The range of salaries is also wide, although, as in the Civil Service, the most highly-paid appointments by no means compare with the highest incomes earned by captains of industry or by leading members of a profession. The actual salary depends on the size and capacity of the local council. The clerk of a large county borough, one of our principal ports or manufacturing towns for instance, will get a salary in the neighbourhood of £5,000 a year. The clerk of a big and busy county council may get similar pay. These are among the leading appointments in local government and compare, in salary, with the highest posts in the civil service. Appointments at salaries above this level are rare. Other professional appointments such as the medical officer of health, architect, or engineer may command a salary of about the same or a little less. The clerk of a smaller borough, or an urban district, may get between £2,000 and £3,000 a year, and the other principal officers slightly less. Some clerks of small authorities get between £1,000 and £1,500 a year.

The salary range for office staff and workpeople compares with salaries paid for similar employment in private commercial firms, but, generally speaking, the tendency is to pay a little less in view of the fact that the appointments are virtually permanent, and carry certain advantages such as sick pay, holidays on full pay, and a pension.

Part-time appointments. A local authority, if it has not enough work to justify making a whole-time appointment for a particular duty, may appoint part-time officers. Some of the smaller urban and rural district councils have part-time clerks, who frequently are local solicitors in private practice. There are part-time medical officers and other medical staff. Sometimes the authority may agree to share the services of an officer; this is particularly the case with medical officers of health, who may, under joint arrangements made between local authorities, be appointed for two or more local government areas. The idea of this is to enable the smaller local authorities to have the services of a medical officer of good standing, while at the same time enabling that officer to receive a salary which will justify the authorities in preventing him from engaging in private practice. Broadly speaking, part-time appointments in local governments are not favoured, although there are cases, e.g., teachers of special subjects such as art and music, where such appointments may be convenient.

Where a solicitor or doctor in private practice is appointed to a part-time appointment, there may be a temptation to let the private professional work interfere with the local authority's work. However conscientious the official may be, it may be difficult for him at all times to reconcile the varying interests – private and public. Similar considerations arise where the official is appointed jointly by two or more authorities. He may not find it easy to serve them both; for the interests of the authorities may on occasions conflict. Accordingly, where an authority can afford to pay a sufficient salary to attract a good officer, and has enough work to keep him occupied whole-time, it is generally found preferable to engage him to serve that authority exclusively.

Voluntary appointments. It is to be noticed that, whereas the law requires that the clerk of a local government authority *must* be a paid official, the legal provisions relating to other appointments are generally to the effect that the local authority *may* pay such remuneration as they think fit, subject of course to the approval, where necessary, of the Government Department concerned. There seems no reason, therefore, why local authorities should not appoint unpaid officers, if such persons can be found. It was at one time not infrequent for the local fire brigade to be run on a voluntary basis, and for all the firemen and officers to have no pay at all. Appointments of this kind are, however, very unusual now, although here and there one may come across a minor appointment (such as a home visitor) with no salary. Such appointments are more of the nature of voluntary social work, of which a very great deal is done in this country, and are hardly to be classed as ordinary official positions. Cases do exist where the office of treasurer to a local authority is filled by a bank, the bank having safe keeping of the council's monies, and making payments to the authority's order, and keeping due account of cash received and paid out. For this the bank may be without any special remuneration.

Fusion of appointments. It was at one time common for a person holding an office under a local authority to hold at the same time various other official appointments. A local solicitor, for instance, might be clerk of the local rural district council, clerk to the poor law guardians, clerk to the school board, as well as being in private practice. This is not now favoured in local government circles. It is allowable for a clerk to a local authority to be also the housing manager. Outside London the clerk of the county council is almost invariably the clerk of the peace, i.e., the clerk of the county quarter sessions. The law provides, however, that the clerk of a local authority may not be the treasurer.

Fusion of compulsory with discretionary appointments is not unusual. For instance the clerk of a local authority is very often the local authority's solicitor; the medical officer of health may also be school medical officer; the surveyor may also be the architect or housing manager, and the inspectors of weights and measures may be the inspectors under the Shops Acts. The registration officers for election purposes are at the same time clerks of local authorities.

The difficulty of finding a person with the necessary technical and professional qualifications for more than one appointment of the higher class itself makes it generally impracticable for one person to hold more than one appointment of any importance.

Pensions. Local authorities generally are compelled to make arrangements for the superannuation of all their whole-time officers. There is provision also for the superannuation, under certain circumstances, of part-time officers and of temporary employees with more than ten years' service.

The details of schemes will vary to some extent in each locality, and with each class of employee. Generally speaking the employee must contribute a fixed percentage of his salary towards the superannuation fund, and the employing authority contributes also to the fund. There may be cases where the employee is not required to contribute at all. Contributions are returned if the employee leaves either through voluntary resignation or by dismissal for inefficiency. In case of dismissal for misconduct, the contributions may be paid to the employee's wife or family.

A pension is generally earned by 10 years' service. Ordinarily an employee must retire at 65, but may retire at 60 if he has served 40 years. In either case he is entitled to a pension. He may also get a pension if he has to retire by reason of ill-health after serving 10 years.

The amount of the pension is based on the average yearly earnings of the last five years before retirement.

In the case of an employee who has contributed to the superannuation fund, the pension will be one-sixtieth of this annual yearly average, multiplied by the number of years which the employee has served. Thus if an employee has earned in his last five years a salary of £500 a year, and has served for 40 years, he will get 40 sixtieths, i.e., two-thirds of £500, that is, about £330 a year pension. In the case of a non-contributing employee, the pension will be half of this. The total pension must not exceed two-thirds of the employee's average annual remuneration.

In addition to the yearly pension, a retiring gratuity or lump sum may be paid. Such a lump sum may also be paid to an employee who has not earned a pension; this sum may not, in general, exceed two years' salary. A pension or gratuity may also be allowed to the widow of an employee who dies before retiring from the service.

Normally a pension dies with the pensioner. It often happens that a man retires, takes his pension, and then dies in a very few years or even months of his retirement, leaving a widow unprovided for. To meet this position, super-annuation schemes may arrange for a man to decide whether to take full pension (which will die with him) or to take a smaller pension (two-thirds is a usual amount) which will be payable to him and, after his death, to his wife. Married women pensioners may have a similar choice.

Interchangeability. One last provision is of importance. If an employee of a local authority is earning pension rights, but leaves the employment of that authority to go into the service of another local authority, arrangements must be made for a 'transfer value' to be paid from the former employing authority to the newly employing authority. In this way a young man entering the service of, say, an urban district council as a junior clerk, may later get a better job as a senior clerk in the office of a borough council. He takes his 'transfer value' to the new employment. A few years afterwards he gets a job as (for instance) deputy clerk to a county council. His 'transfer value' from both his former posts accompanies him to his new post. When he retires, the county council will have to pay him a pension based on all the years of service he has had in local government, starting from his first employment with the urban district council.

The object of this provision is to make for interchangeability of staff between local authorities and to create a nation-wide local government service with prospects open throughout the whole country. In this way an officer in the local government service can gain experience in various areas and build up a wide knowledge, as well as advancing his career, without losing his pension rights. Very many of the leading officials in local government have been in the employment of several local authorities, and this experience is valuable to themselves and to the authorities they serve.

Comparison with the Civil Service. Although the 'transfer value' provisions may tend to stimulate the building up of a national local government service, it must be remembered that the actual terms of employment, choice of candidates, and control and dismissal of local government staff does not rest with any national body, such as a Civil Service Commission or Treasury. The staffing of the civil service, the holding of examinations and the fixing of rates of salary are largely in the hands of those two bodies. In the local government service it is up to the individual local council to settle what rate it will pay, what holidays it will allow, and what hours of work and terms of employment it thinks suitable. This cannot well be otherwise; for conditions differ in various localities. Some councils meet in the day-time, some in the evening. Some meet quarterly, some monthly, and some even fortnightly. Areas differ in size; and the duties of the local councils vary. None the less, apart from the fact that civil service pensions are non-contributory, and the employer of all civil servants is Her Majesty the Queen, there is a great deal of consonance between the practice of the local authorities as employers and that of the civil service. There is the same virtual permanency of employment, salaries are scaled with regular annual increments, staff are grouped into grades, and promotion is made from grade to grade. When making appointments, local authorities not only watch each other's practice, but also have regard to the civil service conditions as far as these are applicable.

Staff representation. Uniformity of practice as between local authorities is to a large measure encouraged by the existence of representative unions of local government employees. The National Association of Local Government Officers has a very wide support among officers of all grades in local government. The workpeople, artisans, park-keepers, porters, hospital attendants, and the like are represented by the ordinary trade unions or special sections of the unions. National and Regional Joint Councils have been set up on which sit representatives of the staffs and the members of local authorities. These Joint Councils discuss conditions of service and agree as to standard conditions which may be adopted (as they generally are) by the employing authorities.

DUTIES OF PRINCIPAL OFFICERS

The Clerk of the Council; The Town Clerk. The clerk of a local authority is the secretary and chief administrative officer. He is somewhat in the position of a managing director of a large firm which has several departments, each with its departmental manager.

The clerk's main function in a modern local government authority is to guide, influence, and manage the whole organization so that it runs in accordance with the legal powers and duties of the authority and in accordance with the policy laid down by the council and its committees. He

156

is captain of the team of departmental managers; he stands as a sort of spokesman between the members of the authority and the official machine; he is the official mouthpiece of the council in its dealings with the general public and the central government; he is the coordinator-in-chief; he is the person to write to if you wish to communicate with the local authority; he conducts the principal official correspondence of the council. He sits in the council chamber, and either in person or by a representative from his department attends all committees, and advises the council and committees as to the proper procedure to follow in conducting business.

He prepares the agenda papers for each meeting, and drafts the minutes of the council and committee. He keeps the formal records of the local authority. He is the general staff manager and advises the council what staff it needs, and what conditions should apply to staff generally.

In most local authorities the clerk is also a solicitor and is responsible for the legal work of the council, dealing with the purchase and sale of property and any parliamentary business such as the promotion of Bills in Parliament to confer powers on the local authority, or seeing that the council's views on other Bills before Parliament are properly stated. In very many cases he has duties in relation to elections, either as registration officer or as returning officer. He may have other duties according to the work or internal organization of his particular council.

The Medical Officer of Health has a very varied set of duties. He is, as his name implies, concerned with the public health of the area of the local authority. Public health has many sides. It includes the sanitation of the area. He generally has under his control a staff of public health inspectors whose duty is to go round and see that houses have proper

157

sanitary arrangements, that no nuisances injurious to health, such as refuse dumps, lack of dust-bins, evil-smelling drains and ditches, or uncontrolled offensive trades exist in the authority's area. The medical officer of health will report on the housing conditions in the area, will make arrangements for preventing infectious diseases, and for the provision of health centres, ambulances, and the other local health services.

If his authority has power to run clinics and similar establishments, he will be responsible for their management, and will advise as to the accommodation and medical and nursing staff required. If his authority has duties in connexion with food inspection and sampling, or analysis, he will be responsible for seeing that these duties are carried out. Maternity and child welfare is in his department. He is generally the school medical officer, and will accordingly be responsible for the periodical inspection and medical examination of school children. He will attend to the decontamination of premises where necessary. Matters relating to the diseases of animals and arrangements for veterinary treatment will come within his sphere. In short his job is to advise his council as to all matters which affect the health of the people.

He has to be highly qualified for his job, and needs special training; for although he must be qualified as a doctor, his duties are hardly those of the general medical practitioner. He must know about disease and how it should be treated; but he has to deal with a range of subjects which are outside the competence of the family physician. Accordingly the law requires that a county medical officer of health must, in addition to being a doctor, hold a diploma in public health, sanitary science, or state medicine. This diploma takes about two years' additional study after he has qualified as a doctor. Medical officers of health of other authorities are also generally required by the Minister of Health to have such a diploma in addition to the ordinary medical qualification.

The Surveyor is usually a qualified professional man, either a surveyor or engineer. He has such duties as the council may impose on him, and is generally concerned with the construction and maintenance of roads and sewers, the collection of refuse, building works, and, in some areas, town planning and housing schemes. His work entails collaboration in many respects with the medical officer of health. For instance the medical officer will report as to what insanitary conditions, or bad housing, or insufficient accommodation for house refuse exist in the area, and it will be the duty of the surveyor to carry out such works to effect any necessary improvements. Sewage disposal works, street cleansing and lighting, and, in some areas, the erection of council houses will be under his charge. He will arrange for these works to be carred out, as the council may decide, either by contract with private firms, or by the employment of labour direct by the council itself. He checks up the bills of quantities and sees that the work is properly done. His duties may also include the repair and maintenance of the council's own buildings, the town hall and offices, schools, and other institutions. Where the council provides public baths or runs a water undertaking, the surveyor may have supervision of these as well.

If the work of the local authority is extensive, the authority may find it necessary to appoint other officers, such as an architect, a highways, or water engineer, or a housing manager. Where such other officers are appointed, they will take on, according to the council's direction, duties which otherwise might be undertaken by the surveyor. The architect for instance will see to the erection of houses and the repair of the council's buildings, and supervise the building by-laws and perhaps also attend to town planning. If there is a housing manager, he will, perhaps, be responsible for the erection of houses and their management; or he may be concerned only with their management after they are built. The creation of such appointments, and the division of work between the officers appointed, varies considerably with each locality.

The Financial Officer, Accountant, Comptroller, or *Treasurer* is, as his title indicates, responsible for keeping the accounts of the local authority. Where (as is sometimes the case) the official treasurer is a bank, the bank will have the duty of keeping the council's money and of making and receiving payments; but there will still be need for a financial officer or accountant in the paid employment of the council to keep the books, examine accounts, make out bills for payment, carry out internal audit, collect income, and give general financial advice to the council and its committees. He must tell the local authority how much money it can spend and afford, what revenues it has available, and, if money is to be borrowed, either by mortgage or by the public issue of stock, he will arrange the matter.

All local authorities are intimately concerned with the making and levying of rates, since a principal part of their income arises out of rates. Accordingly the financial officer will interest himself in rating matters, with assessments and collections, and will advise as to the rate to be levied in each half-year.

The Director of Education or *Education Officer* has many problems which are not always apparent at first sight to the layman. He has to estimate the child population both actual and potential of the area, and arrange for its educational needs in the light of the requirements of the Ministry of Education and of the local council. Since schools once built have to last a number of years, and since teachers take a few years to get trained, and, once trained, need employment for life, the director of education must look ahead, and see that the provision he advises his council to make is neither too extravagant nor too mean, and is capable of adjusting itself to the variations in the child population and their educational needs at varying ages. He must remember that both teachers and children grow older, and he must accordingly allow for a flow of recruits to fill up the classes and the teaching profession.

The arrangements he must make apply not only to primary or elementary education; he must also arrange for the higher education of suitable children, and for their further education either by way of university scholarship, or by suitable technical training. He has also to arrange for adult education by way of evening classes or special schools or polytechnics.

A certain amount of discretion is left to the individual local authority in framing its educational policy, especially as regards higher and technical education. In areas where a particular industry is carried on, such as cotton spinning, wool weaving, coal mining, or ironwork, the local authority may decide to have a special school or classes for technical education in the subjects concerning that industry.

The administration of all these arrangements makes the job of the director of education a busy one. He has human material to deal with, and the efficiency with which he carries out his duties has a great and lasting effect on the children who pass under his care. In some localities the director of education has charge of the museums, art galleries, and libraries managed by the council. On the other hand, some councils appoint separate officers – a Director or Curator of Museums and Art Galleries, or a Chief Librarian – to carry out the work involved in managing such places.

The Local Welfare Officer. This officer has the duty of looking after the needy and disabled either by the provision of residential accommodation for those in need of care and attention, or by providing training and other facilities for the blind and disabled. He has under his control a number of qualified officers, and various local offices where applicants for help can be interviewed, and he has the job of collecting from relatives any necessary contributions towards the maintenance or assistance given. He will also be responsible for the management of the various centres and institutions.

Public Control Officer. Many local authorities have various powers of licensing. Theatres and music-halls, cinemas, nursing homes, massage establishments, employment agencies, petrol filling stations, street trading, motor vehicles, are all examples of instances where a licence from a local authority may be necessary. The local authority, in granting a licence, sees that the premises or persons licensed are fit and proper for the purpose, and may, as a condition of granting the licence, impose requirements which must be complied with by the person holding the licence. These functions are, in a number of localities, the responsibility of a public control officer whose duty will be to advise the council as to the grant of licences, and carry out any necessary investigations into the suitability of applicants. The duties of inspecting weights and measures and of inspecting shops are sometimes given to this officer.

Other principal officers frequently appointed as occasion demands, such as the Chief Officer of Parks, Cemeteries

Manager, Director of the Municipal Bank, or Municipal Theatre, Manager of Baths and Washhouses, or Chief Officer of Municipal Markets have duties which are self-evident from their titles.

The City of London Corporation, in addition to the usual municipal officers, appoints a Chamberlain, who is by ancient custom treasurer of the City, a Vice-Chamberlain who is the Comptroller and City Solicitor and who compiles the rentals of the Corporation's estates and has custody of title deeds, a Remembrancer who attends to the City's parliamentary business, and a Secondary who acts as under-sheriff and compiles the electoral registers.

Legal responsibility of local government Officers. Officers are, of course, the servants of the employing authority, and act under the authority's direction. To some limited extent the duties of some of the principal officers have been described by Act of Parliament. A general duty is laid upon each officer by the Local Government Act, 1933, to account properly for all property and monies of the authority in his charge in connexion with his duties. But, apart from such special instances, the law leaves it to the individual local council to settle exactly what measure of responsibility an officer shall have, how far he may act on his own initiative and to what extent he must get sanction from his council before doing anything on behalf of the council. Some of the larger local authorities place a great deal of responsibility upon their principal officers, giving them a great deal of scope, allowing them to act without previously consulting the council, and enabling them to spend, within certain limits, the council's money in connexion with their official duties.

But apart from whatever duty and responsibility a local government officer has towards his employing council, he has a clear duty towards the public at large. Like the servant of a private master, a local government officer may not commit an illegal act, and claim in defence that he was acting under the orders of the council. In the case of the treasurer this duty to act lawfully in spite of contrary instructions of the council has been specially emphasized. If he receives orders from his council directing him to make an illegal payment he is bound to disobey those orders.[1] If he makes the illegal payment he cannot shelter behind the council's instructions.

Similarly it has been held by the courts that a town clerk who acted under the orders of a mayor, and failed to keep the council fully informed, with the result that money was mis-spent, cannot defend himself by saying that he was under the mayor's instructions. A town clerk, like other local government officers, is appointed to advise the council, and assist in the conduct of public affairs. He stands between the council and the ratepayers and must have regard to the proper position of the local authority in relation to the public as a whole. If he associates himself with any acts of negligence or misconduct he may be surcharged by the auditor (as to which see Chapter 7) and be rendered liable, in the same way as a member who has acted improperly, for any money mis-spent in carrying out those acts.

Interest of officers in contracts. With a view to minimizing possible conflict between an officer's public duty and his private interests, the law provides that an officer who has any interest, direct or indirect, in any contract made or proposed to be made with his council, must disclose that interest by giving notice to the council in writing. If an officer is a shareholder or partner in a firm which has dealings with the council, the officer must disclose the fact. Officers are also forbidden to accept, under colour of their employment, any fees or reward whatsoever, other than their proper remuneration. Failure to comply with any of the foregoing provisions involves a penalty of up to £50 for each offence.

The officer and the elected member. In our system of local government the permanent, paid, expert, whole-time officer is the servant, while the unpaid, part-time, and not always expert member is the master, and has no sure prospect of permanency in office.

Democracy means the right of the electors to choose their own government, and to change that government at will. A member of a local authority is always faced with the likelihood that, at the next election, he may lose his seat on the council, and his place be taken by a newcomer with little or no experience. Although there are many members of local authorities who have spent a lifetime in local government and have gained very extensive experience, none the less local government is, for the elected representative, largely a part-time occupation, whereas for the officer it is a whole-time business. In his particular sphere the officer cannot fail to have a knowledge which the average member is not able to acquire. The member is accordingly in some measure dependent upon the officer.

On the other hand, the officer is dependent upon the member. The member is the master by virtue of his being an elected representative of the local public, and in that capacity he is both lightning conductor and barometer. Any storms of public criticism are discharged upon the member. It is he who loses his seat at the next election if public opinion turns against his policy or actions. The official for the most part shelters behind him.

As a barometer of public opinion the elected member is performing his due and proper function under the democratic mode of government. Under any government, and under democracy most of all, the actions of legislators and governors must rest broadly on the support or sufferance of the people. There is a limit to public patience, beyond which the governor who wishes to avoid trouble must not go. It is the true function of the governor to interpret public feeling, and to enliven it with leadership. It is for the elected members of local authorities to perform this necessary function. The members settle the policy, that is, interpret and assess public feeling and public demands, and the official carries out his job in the light of the policy thus settled. If there were no elected members to interpret public feeling in this way, the official would have to do it for himself. Without periodical elections it would be difficult for an official to do this. How many public officials would welcome standing for election to their posts every three years? Certainly none.

The official and the general public. Much criticism is at times levelled at the public official. The civil servant gets a full measure of this. He is called a bureaucrat, bound up with red tape, unimaginative, slow, and unenterprising. The municipal officer also gets his share of such criticism. There is, of course, one great difference between the civil servant and the municipal officer. A civil servant is not appointed, promoted, or liable to dismissal by the Members of Parliament. The municipal officer on the other hand is directly under the continuous control of the members of his authority. This to some extent has an effect on his demeanour. In his locality he is nearer to the public and their elected representatives. None the less, all officials, whether in Her Majesty's service or in the local government service, have characteristics in common. And they have, like other people, the vices of their virtues. As is only too frequent with all of us, the vices are more often heard of than the virtues.

There are critics who think that the public service would be better if its employment were not permanent, and if officials were more exposed to the likelihood of dismissal. But the feature of permanency has a great value to the public at large. After all, it is the very essence of democratic government that the electors shall be free to change their governments, whether national or local, at will. The fact that the chances and changes of politics do not touch the public official, and that, like the Vicar of Bray, he goes on with his job whatsoever king may reign, ensures continuity of administration. The public servant is the depositary of official experience. So long as he is permanent and independent of politics, so long can his advice be unbiased.

In entering the public service he has renounced the opportunity of seeking those glittering prizes which can be won by the successful business man. For his qualifications he receives less than he might earn in non-public employment, yet he is expected to be unbribable, to devote his best energies to the public service while getting little of the glamour of public acclamation that seems to be one of the attractions of being an elected representative. The official must watch the interests of the public at large, be wise in his judgements, be as painstaking as a trustee, exert a balancing influence upon the enthusiasm of his political masters, remain honourable and relatively unambitious and largely anonymous. To satisfy all these exacting requirements he has to be a person of a certain type.

The best of our public officials do not, in a sense, work for the salaries they earn; they get a high degree of self-expression and a great deal of moral satisfaction out of the fact that they are there to serve the public, not for profit, but for the general good. The public servant is by no means a dull fellow. He is educated and intelligent. If, as a rule, he seems hesitant and unadventurous, it is because, from the nature of his work, with so many public claims to reconcile, he cannot well act otherwise. If (there are of course always exceptions) he seems detached and slightly theoretical in his approach, with somewhat of an old-time professional air, with a trifle less hardness of manner than some occupations seem to evoke, it is because he is the only type of person who has the temperament for being satisfied with the circumscribing conditions under which his duties have to be carried out.

He makes his due, faithful, and necessary contribution to the public welfare, and has great pride in doing so. The service that he gives is sincere and uninfluenced by ulterior private motive. A trustworthy and uncorrupt public service is taken for granted in this country; it constitutes a public benefit not lightly to be disregarded.

CHAPTER 7

WHERE DOES THE MONEY COME FROM?

It does not all come out of the rates. It is common to suppose that the expenditure of local authorities comes out of the rates. This may be due to the publicity given at council elections to questions relating to the rates. It may be also due to the fact that, formerly, only ratepayers could vote at local government elections. Since 1945, however, all persons (ratepayers or not) residing in a local government area may vote at such elections. This alteration in the local government franchise was justified by the fact that the expenditure of local government authorities on revenue account is now very largely subsidized by grants from the central government. In fact, in recent decades, the total amount of government grants to local authorities has approached and even exceeded the total income from rates of all the local authorities throughout the country. Local authorities in some cases have been spending more money that is taxpayers' money than money that is ratepayers' money.

Borrowed money. On capital account, the government grants amount to only a small percentage of the total capital expenditure of local authorities. But the general practice of local authorities is to pay for the bulk of such expenditure out of borrowed money. This practice was defended by the argument that to construct, for instance, a new road or housing estate out of current income would not only impose a large expense on current rates, but would have the effect of conferring upon posterity a benefit to which it would make no contribution. If a road is to last in perpetuity, why should not succeeding generations bear a share of the cost? Accordingly, it is common to meet expenditure of this kind by a loan to be repaid over a long term of years.

Alarm has sometimes been expressed at the propensity of local authorities to meet expenditure out of loans. As in the case of the national debt, the interest on the borrowed money itself constitutes a very substantial charge on the borrowing authority. And if the practice of borrowing is persisted in, local authorities end up with a huge current obligation to pay interest. In fact, the total amount of loan charges of local authorities throughout the country is something like half the total income from rates. In other words, looking at the matter from the point of view of the country as a whole, about half the money raised from rates goes on paying for the debts of the past.

Conditions vary, of course, with each local authority. And it must be borne in mind that a very great deal of the money borrowed, like the money raised by shares or debentures by a commercial company, is spent on buildings, mains, and permanent works of one kind or another, which help to produce income and, when the debt is paid off, represent valuable assets.

Other income. Apart from rates and government grants, local authorities have certain income from fees charged for such matters as the issue of licences, the use of swimming-baths, and games facilities, from rents of property owned by the authority, and, where a trading undertaking is carried on, such as a municipal market or transport service, there is an income from receipts. The total income of local authorities throughout the country from receipts other than rates and grants is equal to about half that arising from rates.

170

It will be seen, then, that the actual amount of money raised by rates is by no means the main source of a local authority's income. Taking local authorities as a whole, and leaving aside capital expenditure, only about two fifths of their expenditure is borne directly out of rates.

Use of income to relieve the rates. As a general rule, the profit income of a local authority from property or from trading undertakings can be used to assist in meeting the cost of non-remunerative services, although it has been argued that profits from a trading undertaking ought to go back into that undertaking, so as to reduce the charges made to the consumer for the service rendered.

THE RATING SYSTEM

Difference between rates and taxes. Taxes, particularly income tax, may be regarded as a compulsory contribution to national expenditure, the amount of the contribution of the individual taxpayer being measured according to his capacity to pay. No account is taken, in assessing or collecting the taxes, of the particular benefit which the individual taxpayer will receive for his contribution.

In the case of rates, the underlying conception is (or used to be) somewhat different. Rates have been regarded as contributions towards local services, the individual ratepayer's contribution being measured by the benefit which he receives. In the days when local services consisted mainly of highways, bridges, and sewerage, it was, in the main, fair, as a rough and ready method, to assess a person for rates on the basis of the property he owned or occupied. The more land he had, the greater use would he make of the roads and sewers. In later times the assumption could be made that a man who occupied a big house had a big income to correspond, and got a corresponding benefit from local services. This principle of matching the contribution to the benefit received is illustrated by the fact that agricultural land pays no rates, and industrial property pays only a half of the normal rates. This can be justified because such land and property get little or no benefit from the social services which absorb the greater part of a local authority's income.

As these social services have expanded, the notion that the ratepayer's contribution can be measured by the benefit he gets has become absurd. Nowadays, in fact, the poorest and neediest get the most out of the rates and make the least contribution, whereas the occupiers of 'good-class' property, especially commercial property, get little benefit at all in proportion to the rates they pay.

Rates have nowadays become in fact a sort of local tax on the occupation of property. This being so, critics have asserted that rating is unfair, in that the value of the property (for instance, a shop) occupied by a person bears no relation at all to that person's capacity to pay, and no real relation to the services he gets from the local authority.

Besides this, in the poor and distressed areas, where the values of property are low and the ratepaying capacity of the population is also low, the rate income has no relation to the needs of the area as regards social services. In fact, the poorest areas, like the poorest individuals, require, by modern standards, more services than the areas which are more fortunately placed. For all these reasons rating has even been called an 'unjust tax'. Government grants do in a great measure help to balance up the inequalities; but none the less, there is general agreement that the rating system is by no means ideal.

Rating authorities. Since rates are based upon the occupation of land or premises, an essential step in the making of a rate is the valuation of the property. The whole country is divided up into 'rating areas' over which there are 'rating authorities'. These authorities are, in fact, the councils of boroughs, urban, and rural districts. County councils and parish councils are not rating authorities. The business of a rating authority is to make and levy rates as required.

Assessment. Each piece of land, each building, etc., subject to rates and separately occupied is known as a 'hereditament'. Each hereditament is given an 'annual value' which is supposed to be the rent which a tenant from year to year might reasonably be expected to pay, the tenant paying rates and taxes, and the landlord paying for repairs and insurance. This business of valuation is not always easy, especially in the case of industrial properties not likely to be let at a rent, such as mines, canals, waterworks, and docks. The mode of arriving at annual values is often artificial and arbitrary, and, even in the case of house property does not, in some areas, bear any true relation to the actual rent that a tenant may pay.

The rateable properties of the nationalized gas and electricity undertakings are valued in a special manner in which output and consumption are taken into account, and the total rateable value of each gas and electricity authority is then apportioned among the rating areas within the area of operations.

The nationalized railways are not liable for rates, but sums are paid in lieu of rates by the British Transport Commission to the Central Government and distributed among the rating authorities.

Rates are levied on the occupier. In the case of premises let on lease, the tenant, and not the owner, pays the rates. Because of this, the value for rating purposes is, in certain cases, e.g., dwelling houses and land, reduced below the 'annual value'. As said above, the annual value is arrived at on the assumption that the landlord pays for repairs and insurance. He would accordingly allow for this in fixing the rent and make it high enough to meet those expenses. The measure of the occupier's liability is, however, the net rent, i.e., the annual value less the cost of repairs and insurance. Accordingly the law requires that from the 'annual value' or 'gross value' there shall be made certain specified deductions for these items. The value so arrived at is the 'net annual value' or 'rateable value'.

What is an occupier? Occupation for rating purposes includes actual possession of the property with some degree of permanence. Accordingly a mere temporary holding of land will not constitute rateable occupation. Nor is a lodger or a guest liable to rates. There must be some actual or presumed benefit from the occupation – the occupation must be beneficial. Consequently an empty house to which the tenant has no immediate intention of returning bears no rates, although if the tenant intends to return at any time, and is thus holding the premises in that prospect, that will constitute rateable occupation. If the house has no tenant, the landlord becomes the legal occupier, but if he tries to find a tenant but cannot, the owner's occupation will not incur liability to rates, because such occupation is not beneficial.

Valuation lists are issued by the valuation officers of the Inland Revenue once every five years. These lists show the values placed upon properties in the rating area. The necessary information to make up the list is obtained from owners, and the list is sent to the rating authority and open to public inspection.

Objections to valuation: Amendments. Every person who is aggrieved by the list, either because he has been over-rated, or because other occupiers have been under-rated in comparison, may make an objection to the valuation officer. This officer may himself alter the list. The objector, if still unsatisfied, may agree to refer the matter to arbitration or may appeal to a local Valuation Court sitting in public. There is a further right of appeal from these Courts to the Lands Tribunal.

The valuation lists may be altered in the course of any five-year period to accord with changes of circumstance, such as the demolition or alteration or new construction of premises.

Precepts. A rating authority has to meet out of rates not only its own expenditure as a local government authority – it has to meet the expenses of certain other authorities as well. The expenses of the metropolitan police, for instance, are met out of the rates levied by rating authorities throughout the police area. The expenses of county councils also are borne out of the rates collected by the rating authorities in the county. The expenses of certain joint boards, and, to some extent, parish councils and parish meetings are met in a similar way. All these authorities issue demands, known as 'precepts', upon the rating authorities.

County councils and the metropolitan police authorities work out what their expenditure would mean in terms of an actual rate of so much in the pound of the total rateable value of the whole area, and then ask each of the rating authorities to levy a rate of that amount. This method ensures that each local rating area bears a proper share, according to its rateable value, of the total expense. In the case of counties the position is a little complicated by the fact that in some local areas the local district council provides services which in other areas are provided by the county council.

County expenditure is therefore divided into two classes – 'general county expenses' to which all parts of the county contribute and 'special county expenses' to which only certain parts of the county contribute. On somewhat the same principle, expenditure in rural areas incurred in respect of particular parishes is designated as 'special expenses' which can be collected by the rural district council from those particular parishes (unless the district council decides, as it may, to treat some or all of these special expenses as general expenses chargeable over the whole district). This means that the rating authority has to make differential rates – a 'general rate' upon the whole of its area for expenditure incurred for the benefit of the whole area, and a 'special rate' or the collection of 'special expenses' in respect of particular expenditure incurred on behalf of individual localities.

In addition to these complications, there are, in most areas, various properties which are wholly or partly exempt from rates, e.g., Government property, churches, and chapels, and certain types of property in respect of which concessions have been granted under various Acts of Parliament.

Making the rate. When the rating authority has done all the necessary (and rather involved) calculation, and has also formed an estimate of its own expenditure, it works out how much to collect from each rateable occupier. The amount required is expressed as so much in the pound of rateable value and is generally levied for each half-year. Thus if the half-yearly rate is 5s in the £ (10s for the year), an occupier of property rated at £40 a year will pay in each half year £10 in rates (£20 a year). The demand note for the rate must show the purposes for which the rate is required and for what authorities the rate is being collected. In the case of small properties, e.g. blocks of tenements, the rating authority may agree to let the owner collect the rates from the tenants. Under such an arrangement known as 'compounding' the owner gets a discount.

The remedy against a person who fails to pay rates is by distress, i.e., by seizing the furniture or other property on the premises, and, if this is insufficient, the defaulter may be imprisoned.

GOVERNMENT GRANTS

The practice of subsidizing local authorities by money provided by Parliament out of national taxes has grown up in the last hundred years as a means of compensating local authorities for various burdens, obligations, and requirements imposed on them by the Central Government. Where a new service has been instituted or improved, such as public education, the building of main roads or the provision of working-class houses, the Government made a practice of contributing in various ways to the cost involved. The view was taken that where a public service, such as state education, can be regarded as being more for national than for strictly local benefit, it is right that the state should bear part of the cost.

As has been pointed out earlier in this chapter, the rate income of local authorities varies considerably. The poorer areas where the bulk of the population are at a low income level, and property values are also low, are the very areas where the greatest amount of public service is required. The result has been that these needy areas have not the means to provide out of the rates the services they want. Consequently it has been necessary for the Central Government to subsidize the local authorities.

An additional reason for the payment of grants to local authorities has been that Parliament has itself interfered with the rate income of local authorities by exempting certain classes of property owners from the obligation to pay rates. Thus no rates are payable in respect of agricultural land, and only one half of the normal rates is paid in respect of industrial and freight transport hereditaments. These concessions, granted by Parliament in pursuance of a national policy, have necessitated some compensation to local authorities for the consequent loss of rate income. The answer has been grants from the Government.

Development of grants in aid. It is not intended to enter into a detailed discussion here about the history of the various methods by which local authorities have been subsidized by the Central Government. But a brief reference to history may be of interest. The first grants were made in 1835 and were in respect of the cost of the transportation overseas of prisoners convicted at assizes and quarter sessions. The amount of grant was proportioned to the actual expenditure of the local authority under this head. Later on, grants of one fourth, later enlarged to one half, of the cost of pay and clothing of local police forces were made.

It is to be noticed that the grants made in this early period were based on a proportion or percentage of the actual total expenditure of the individual local authority in respect of the service in question. The grant paid was subject to the government being satisfied that the service was efficient and properly provided. Accordingly, the grant system gave the Central Government a certain control and influence over the activities of the local authorities.

Assigned revenues. In 1888, when county councils and county borough councils were first set up, it was felt to be reasonable to divert to the use of local authorities certain state taxes arising from the areas of those authorities. The idea was that, as the local area became more prosperous, the proceeds from those taxes would correspondingly increase, and help the local authority to provide expanding services in accordance with local needs. There was a certain amount of difficulty in ascertaining how much of the particular state taxes arose in each area, and how to apportion the revenue from those taxes among the individual local authorities.

The taxes selected for this form of treatment, by reason of their local character and the prospect of their increase with expanding prosperity, were the licence duties on male servants, armorial bearings, dogs, etc., a share of the probate and estate duties, and the surtaxes upon beer and spirits. The inclusion of the latter item in the list accounts for the statement that is sometimes made that, when county and county borough councils in 1902 were made responsible for higher education, the necessary funds were provided out of liquor duties.

Additional percentage grants. The assigned revenues were in fact found insufficient to meet the expanding expenditure of local authorities upon new and enlarged services which came into vogue at the end of the 19th century. Accordingly, further financial assistance to local authorities was necessary. The older system of making grants on a percentage of the actual expenditure on a particular service was resorted to. The amount of these percentage grants, made to individual local authorities in respect of such services as education, housing, and roads, varied according to the local conditions, and served both to stimulate the provision of services, and to give the Central Government (by the threat of withholding grant) the means to ensure that services were efficiently carried on.

Effect of percentage grants. Critics of the system of percentage grants have suggested that this type of grant encourages extravagance. Although the gross expenditure has in general to be approved before the grant can be claimed, local councils (it is said) may tend, when considering a scheme of operations, to have regard to the fact that a substantial portion of the cost will be reimbursed from national funds. This may induce the council to go in for a scale of expenditure which, while it may be justifiable on the ground of public service, would not be on the same scale if the local council had to foot the bill entirely itself.

A further criticism of the percentage grant is that it subjects the local council to the scrutiny of the central department concerned, which does not always appreciate the intimate needs of the locality.

A major criticism is that percentage grants do not take fully into account the needs and financial capacity of a local area. If a council can meet in the first place the cost of providing a service, and get a part of the expenditure repaid by the Government, this may go far to meet the local needs. But supposing the local council is so poor that it cannot find its due share of the expenditure? In such a case the promise of a government percentage grant of ordinary proportions will not really meet that case. What is needed there is an abnormal percentage, or even perhaps a reimbursement of the total.

The Block grant. When Parliament granted relief from rates to agriculture and industry, the result was to reduce the rate income as a whole in each local government area. The loss of income was not applicable to any particular services, but was a general loss affecting all services. Moreover, since the amount of agricultural and industrial property varied in each case, and the value of such property varied as well, it was necessary to find a suitable method of compensating local authorities in accordance with the needs of the case. A formula was devised with a view to measuring the claims of each area, and, on the basis of that formula, 'block grants' were paid to local authorities, not in respect of any particular service, but as a subsidy towards their general expenses. The Local Government Act, 1929, which instituted this formula and the system of block grants, did away with most of the former percentage grants, and to a large extent abolished the system of assigned revenues.

General and rate-deficiency grants. The Local Government Act, 1948, abolished the 'block grant' and introduced a new form of government assistance to local authorities – the 'Exchequer Equalization Grants' payable to local authorities whose rateable value was below the national average as ascertained and weighed by a special formula.

The Local Government Act, 1958, went a stage further in an attempt to adjust the financial relations between central and local government. This Act abolished many of the percentage grants then remaining (including those for education, the fire service, local health services, the care of 'deprived children' and certain town planning matters) and substituted 'General Grants' in lieu. The scheme of Exchequer Equalization Grants was amended by the substitution of a system of 'Rate Deficiency Grants'.

Amount of the General Grants. The annual aggregate amount of the General Grants is prescribed in advance by a General Grant Order made by the Minister of Housing and Local Government and confirmed by Parliament. Such an Order will cover a period of not less than two years.

The aggregate so prescribed will be distributed among local authorities by way of 'basic grants' and 'supplementary grants'. Each basic grant will be ascertained by reference to the population and the number of children in the area of the recipient authority. The formula for the distribution of the supplementary grants will take into account the number of old people, the school population, the density of population and any recent decline in it, the road mileage, and (in the case of authorities in Greater London) the higher level of prices and costs in and around London.

The underlying notion of all this is to make some attempt, if only in an arbitrary and somewhat artificial fashion, to bring the grants into accord with the local needs and local conditions. In fixing the annual aggregate of the General Grants, the Minister is required by the Act of 1958 to take into account the latest information about expenditure on local services, the levels of and foreseeable variations in prices, costs, and remuneration, probable fluctuations in the demand for the services, and the general economic conditions.

A local authority is free to spend its General Grant on any service it wishes, and not necessarily on those services for which percentage grant has formerly been paid. Since the General Grant is not therefore specifically related to any particular item or project (as was formerly the case with percentage grants) the local authorities can be said to have a greater freedom under this new system of grants.

None the less, the Central Government, as guardians of the nation's economic life, must keep watch over the spending activities of local authorities by requiring the submission of programmes of capital expenditure, proposals for financing local schemes by borrowing, and reports and returns of expenditure. In this way, the Central Government will be able to see generally how local authorities are behaving.

Moreover, if a local authority fails to achieve or maintain reasonable standards in the provision of the services in respect of which the General Grant has replaced the former percentage grants, the appropriate Minister may report to Parliament recommending that the grant be reduced.

Payment of Rate-deficiency Grants is made to any local authority, other than a parish council, where the product of a penny rate for the authority's area is less than the 'standard penny rate product' for that area. The 'standard penny rate product' for the area bears the same proportion to the product of a penny rate over the whole of England and Wales, as does the population of the local area bear to the total population of England and Wales.

The amount of the Rate Deficiency Grant is related to the normal expenditure of the authority in the same ratio as the actual penny rate product bears to the 'standard penny rate product', the idea being to bring the local rate product up to the national standard.

In the Administrative County of London there are special arrangements for adjusting the precepts of the London County Council upon the metropolitan borough councils (the rating authorities) so as to equalize to some extent the financial burdens falling upon the poorer boroughs.

Present percentage grants. These are paid in respect of police, roads, and various other matters. The police grant is 50 per cent of the local authority's expenditure on this service, subject to the Home Secretary's being satisfied that the service is efficient.

In regard to roads and bridges the Government makes grants on a percentage basis to local authorities towards the expense of building new routes, improving old ones, maintenance, and repair. The provision of pedestrian crossing-places, subways, road signs, guard-rails, and tree-planting are among the items for which grants may be paid. The grants have varied from time to time and according to the type of work in respect of which expenditure has been incurred. Percentages from 20 to 75 have been paid.

Present assigned revenues. As a result of various alterations in the law, the assigned revenues to local authorities are much reduced. County and county borough councils may collect and keep the duties on guns, game licences, and dogs. This is the last remnant of the system. These authorities also collect the duties on motor cars and driving licences, but the money received has to be handed over to the Government, which reimburses the councils the costs of collection.

Housing grants. In respect of housing and slum clearance, the method of providing financial assistance to local authorities has varied from time to time according to national policy, financial resources, and housing needs. One method of paying grant has been to reimburse the local authority its approved expenditure over a fixed minimum, e.g., the annual loss in excess of a rate of 1d in the £. Another method has been the 'unit cost' system under which the grant is fixed at so much in respect of each person re-housed, or at so much in respect of each dwelling erected. Grants have been payable at rates varying from £5 10s. to £12 yearly for 40 or 60 years for each house erected, and up to £50 or more for each flat in a high block. This enables the local authority to pay off money borrowed for housing operations, and helps towards the expense of maintenance.

The 'unit cost' type of grant avoids certain of the disadvantages of the percentage grant, in that the 'unit cost' grant is fixed, and, not being based on expenditure, does not tend to extravagance. Although the local authority's housing proposals require general government approval, the making of the grant does not entail continuing detailed supervision by the Government Department concerned. This type of grant has, however, the disadvantage of not being adjustable to meet varying price levels in different parts of the country, although provision has been made in some cases, e.g., where the housing is in rural areas and transport costs are high, or in areas where building land is exceptionally expensive, for the grant to be higher than the normal.

What of the future? The attempts made since 1929 to alter the methods by which the Central Government gives financial aid to local authorities point to the likelihood that the problems of local government finance will never be static, to be settled once for all. Changes in social conditions bring changes in the need for local services. The pulsations in the nation's economic life, and variations in government policies will all have some reflection in the financial attitudes of central and local authorities.

Apart from the fact that the nation, the local authorities, and indeed the private citizens are never likely to have enough money for all the things that money can be properly spent on, the main difficulty about local government finance is that the rating system is not adequate as a mode of financing local government.

Alternative and additional methods have often been suggested and examined. A local income tax, and local taxes of other kinds have been canvassed, but none of them have found general acceptance. The rating system still persists as a feature embedded in national tradition. It has its great advantages. Valuation is simple to assess, and cannot be dodged; for it is based on physical property which is manifestly in existence. No returns of income are required. Rates are levied on the occupier, who is on the spot, and not on an absent owner who may not be easy to trace.

The rating system provides local authorities with a financial link between the elector-ratepayer and the elected member; it exemplifies the established British principle of 'no taxation without representation', and, in so far as the ratepayers are electors and 'consumers' of the local authority's services, it allows for representation both of those who pay for and those who benefit by these services.

No other system which displays all these features has yet been discovered. The rating system is therefore, in spite of its shortcomings, likely to remain with us permanently. In consequence, the problem of how best to supplement the rating system by other public subventions, such as government grants, will also remain.

CONTRIBUTIONS BY COUNTY COUNCILS TO OTHER COUNCILS

A county council is empowered to make any contribution it thinks fit towards the expenditure of the council of a non-county borough or urban or rural district within the county, and may also contribute towards the expenditure on public open spaces by a parish council or by a borough which has been included in a rural district (as to which see Chapter 9).

BORROWING BY LOCAL AUTHORITIES

Power to borrow. All local authorities have power to raise money by loan for buying land, providing buildings, executing works, or providing plant for the purpose of carrying out their legal functions. County councils may borrow in order to lend to parish councils. The mode of borrowing may be (i) by mortgage, (ii) by the issue of stock, or (iii) by the issue of debentures.

Sanction to loans. These borrowing powers may be exercised only with the consent of some superior authority, called the 'loan sanctioning authority'. Loans for public transport purposes require the sanction of the Minister of Transport.

In other cases local authorities must seek the prior sanction of the Minister of Housing and Local Government.

The London County Council itself is in an unusual position. Each year it promotes in Parliament a special private Bill which, when passed, becomes the London County Council (Money) Act for that year. The Act says how much money the Council may spend on capital account. This sum may be borrowed, either by mortgages, the issue of bonds, by bills of exchange (London County Bills), by terminable annuities, by the temporary use of sinking or other reserve funds, or (the most usual) by the issue of London County Stock. The Act also says how much money the Council may lend to other local authorities, e.g., Metropolitan Borough Councils. The Treasury is the central Department exercising supervision over the financial operations of the London County Council.

Period of loans. The law provides that loans by local authorities must be repaid within a certain period. The period varies with the different purposes. For most purposes sixty years is a usual period. In other cases the period may vary from thirty to eighty years.

All securities created by a local authority for loan purposes are charged upon all the revenues of the local authority. Those securities issued since 1 January 1934, rank equally, without any priority.

FINANCIAL PROCEDURE

Annual estimates. All county councils are required by law to frame an annual budget of income and expenditure. The Finance Committee prepares this budget and submits it to the council before the beginning of each financial year. Other authorities are not actually required to frame a budget, but in practice they do. Indeed, they can hardly avoid doing so;

for it is essential for the authority to know what its financial needs are for the forthcoming year, in order that the necessary rates may be made and levied.

A general practice is for each committee to make an estimate of its probable expenditure for the forthcoming year, and to pass this on to the Finance Committee, who then make up a total budget and submit it to the Council for approval.

A local authority does not, like many private persons, find out what income it has and then trim its expenditure so as to keep within its income. A local authority finds out what money it needs and what income it may expect, and then sets out to make up the difference out of the rates.

Spending procedure. When the estimates are approved by the Council they constitute an expression of the Council's intentions. They do not in themselves necessarily constitute authority to spend the money estimated.

It is a frequent practice of local authorities to divide up the annual estimates among the various committees in respect of the services controlled by each committee, and to give each committee authority to spend, up to the amount provided in the estimates, such sums as may be required. All this is usually arranged in the council's standing orders. It is sometimes a requirement that any sums over a certain amount must not be spent until the council's finance committee or the full council has approved the spending of that particular sum.

Accordingly, when, for instance, the local authority needs a new motor lorry, the officer in charge of the service in question will report the fact to the committee concerned. The committee will then ascertain if there is sufficient money in the estimates for this expenditure. If there is, the committee will then refer to the standing orders, to see if it can spend the money itself, or whether the council must be asked to give authority for the money to be spent. If there is no provision in the estimates, then a supplemental estimate may be necessary, submitted (if the council's financial procedure so requires) through the Finance Committee to the full council.

The council's financial procedure may provide for officers to have authority to spend money on certain items and up to certain limits, in which case no separate authority will be required, but a periodical account by the officer will be necessary.

Accounts. All local authorities are under a general legal obligation to deal in a proper way with the money under their control. It is public money, and if it is improperly applied, proceedings may be taken by the Attorney-General against the authority itself or against individual members or officers. All local authorities are, further, required by law to keep proper accounts and deal efficiently with receipts and payments. They (with the exception of parish councils) must set up a general fund, called the 'general rate fund' or 'county fund' as the case may be, to and from which all receipts and expenses must be paid.

The accounts are in most cases complicated by the fact that certain expenses are not chargeable over the whole of the authority's area. Accordingly county councils must keep separate accounts of 'general county expenses' and 'special county expenses' (which are borne only by certain parts of the county). Similarly rural district councils in whose areas certain parishes are chargeable with expenditure incurred specially for them, must keep a 'general district account' applicable to the whole district, and a 'special district account' dealing with the special expenses of individual parishes.

Parish authorities are not required to set up a general fund; but their financial procedure is subject to definite legal rules. A parish council may, in general, spend up to the amount of a rate of 4d in the pound of the rateable value of the parish, but the parish meeting may authorize expenditure up to 8d in the pound. The Minister of Housing and Local Government may increase these limits. Every cheque or order for payment must be signed by two members of the parish council. If there is no parish council, the chairman of the parish meeting is responsible for the expenditure and must keep proper accounts.

AUDIT

District Auditor: Surcharge. The accounts of all local authorities are made up annually, normally to 31 March, and, with the exception of certain accounts of boroughs outside London, are subject to audit by the District Auditor, a government official. The audit is advertised beforehand, and the accounts of the local authority are made available for public inspection. Any ratepayer may raise, before the District Auditor, objection to any item in the accounts.

The auditor must look not only at the accuracy of the accounts. He must go into the legality of all the items. If he is dissatisfied as to the legality of any item, his duty is to strike that item out of the accounts. He may then surcharge the item upon the members who voted for the spending of the money making up the item. He may similarly surcharge officers by whose carelessness or dereliction of duty money has been mis-spent or improperly applied. Persons surcharged thereupon become liable at law to repay the money out of their own pockets to the council. To enforce repayment, a distress warrant may be issued and the property of the person liable may be seized.

The law provides, however, that there shall be no surcharge if the Minister of Housing and Local Government has previously sanctioned the expenditure in question. Accordingly, local authorities in doubt as to their legal powers generally obtain prior sanction from the Minister. This sanction will avoid a surcharge, but it does not necessarily make the payment legal. The legality of the payment might still be challenged by action in the courts by any person interested.

Surcharge for a sum over £500 disqualifies a person from being a member of a local authority for five years.

Appeal can be made against a surcharge. If the amount involved is over £500, appeal lies to the High Court. In other cases the appeal is decided by the Minister. Alternatively application may be made to the Court or to the Minister by the person surcharged for remission of the surcharge on the grounds that he acted reasonably and ought fairly to be excused.

Borough Audit. The accounts of boroughs outside London in respect of education and certain other specially prescribed services are audited by the District Auditor in any case; but other accounts may be audited in various ways according to the desire of the individual borough council.

First, the council may decide to submit all its accounts to the District Auditor, in which case the provisions as to objections, surcharges, appeals, etc., come into effect.

Secondly, the borough council may decide to appoint a professional auditor, who must be properly qualified. He has no power of surcharge. He may be paid.

Lastly, if the borough council comes to no special decision, the old-fashioned method of borough audit applies.

Under this system, there are three auditors, two of them being elected annually by the borough electors, and one being appointed by the mayor from among the members of the council. They may have no professional qualifications whatever, their powers are limited, and they have no power of surcharge.

In either of the cases where audit is not conducted by the District Auditor, the borough treasurer when the audit is complete must print and publish an abstract of the accounts.

Local financial returns. Annual returns of income and expenditure are required to be sent by all local authorities to the Minister of Housing and Local Government. From these returns the Ministry is able to compile necessary statistics, and to exercise oversight in regard to the general financial operations of local authorities.

CHAPTER 8

SUPERVISION AND CONTROL OVER LOCAL AUTHORITIES

IT will have been gathered, from what has already been said, that the Central Government has a considerable interest in the doings of local government authorities, and is not without a very great influence over their activities. This central control is necessary because the carrying on of the services for which local authorities are responsible is to a large extent a national affair. It is advisable, for instance, that the education of the children throughout the country should conform to accepted standards, and that the schools and teaching in one area should not be substantially inferior to those of other areas. Similar considerations apply to other services. The government having, through Parliament, placed upon local authorities various duties and responsibilities, is entitled, and obliged, to keep under supervision the work of local authorities in carrying out those duties and responsibilities.

It is not only essential that steps should be taken to see that local authorities perform efficiently the jobs they have been given to do; it is also essential that the local authorities should not exceed their duties by engaging in ventures for which they have no legal authority.

Accordingly, the methods by which the doings of local authorities are kept under control fall into two main classes: (a) Ministerial control, by a Minister of State or a Government Department on his behalf; (b) judicial control, exercised through the courts of justice. There are also cases (*c*) where control can be exercised by one local authority over another.

(A) MINISTERIAL CONTROL

(i) *Grants*. Control by a Minister or a Department can be exercised in various ways. Government Departments concerned with the payment of government grants towards local services are able, by the threat of withholding grant, to exercise supervision over those services. The General Grants and the percentage grants are all given on the basis that the Minister concerned shall be satisfied with the efficiency of the local authority's service or with the work for which the grant is to be paid.

(ii) *Loan sanction*. Again, when a local authority wishes to borrow money there is always need for some higher authority, generally the Minister of Housing and Local Government, to give sanction to the proposed loan. Before giving sanction, the loan-sanctioning authority has to be satisfied that the purpose for which the money is required is proper, and that the amount to be borrowed is reasonable and necessary.

(iii) *Audit and surcharge*. The powers of the District Auditor to scrutinize the accounts of a local authority and to surcharge improper expenditure upon the members authorizing that expenditure provide an example of central government control. Surcharges can be avoided either by getting the prior sanction of the Minister of Housing and Local Government to the expenditure, or by appealing to him for remission (see Chapter 7).

(iv) *Default powers*. Some Acts of Parliament which impose a duty on local authorities make provision to deal with the case where a local authority does not carry out that duty. For instance if a local authority fails to provide proper sewers or sewage disposal plant, or if it does not take such steps as it should to put an end to smoke nuisance, the appropriate Minister may declare the local authority to be in default. If the Minister of Education finds that a local education authority has not provided the education service which it ought, he may make a similar declaration.

The consequences which follow from the declaration of default are various.

Thus if a local authority fails to do its duty in relation to public health the Minister may, after due inquiry, direct the local authority to do such things within such time and in such manner as the Minister may specify. If the Minister's order is not complied with the members of the local authority may all be arrested. This drastic step is, however, seldom taken and has fortunately seldom been necessary.

And if a local authority having power to make building by-laws fails to do so, the Minister may himself make by-laws for the area of the defaulting authority.

Further, cases may arise in which a district council fails to do its proper job. The Minister may give the job to the county council to do at the expense of the defaulting district council. In some instances, under special powers, the Minister may deal with the default by suspending the local authority altogether and by putting in an official to carry out the local duties under the Minister's direction in the place of the local authority.

In certain public health matters the London County Council, if satisfied that a Metropolitan Borough Council is in default, may perform any acts which the borough council ought to have performed and may charge the borough council with the expenses.

The law relating to education provides an example of the extension of the principle of default powers to cover a case, not where the local authority have failed or refused to act, but where they have acted and have acted improperly. The law provides that, if any local education authority acts or proposes to act unreasonably in carrying out its duties in relation to education, the Minister may give directions accordingly. Apparently such directions may be enforced by legal process.

(v) *Administrative appeals.* Various Acts of Parliament have provisions which enable persons who may be adversely affected by the acts of a local authority to appeal to a Minister. For instance, a person whose property is affected by a planning scheme may make an appeal to the Minister of Housing and Local Government. The Minister may override the decision of the local authority. The prospect of such appeals tends to have a certain guiding effect on the town planning operations of the local authority. It is easily appreciated that if the local authority goes on losing, or winning, appeals of this kind, the result will be to bring the policy of the local authority into eventual harmony with the policy of the Ministry.

Appeals may also be made to a Minister in respect of proposals for the compulsory purchase of land, in respect of certain matters relating to the provision of sewers, in respect of the restrictions imposed by a local authority, in respect of 'ribbon development' along highways, in respect of interference with private property by electricity suppliers, and various other matters.

Sometimes an Act of Parliament will say that a Minister, on complaint being made to him, may take action to deal with the complaint; sometimes an Act provides that persons aggrieved by the operations of a local authority may make objections to a Minister. In such cases a usual course for the Minister to take is to direct one of the officials of the

Ministry to hold a public local inquiry – a sort of court, held in some premises in the locality, at which interested parties may state their objections.

(vi) *Consent of a Minister*. In some cases the activities of a local authority require approval of a Minister before the local authority's intentions can legally be carried out. As mentioned in Chapter 6 certain Ministers have an interest in and control over certain staff appointments.

By-laws made by a local authority require the approval in some form or other of a Government Department.

(vii) *Regulations*. Ministers are often given power by Act of Parliament to make regulations indicating how certain powers are to be exercised. This kind of power is very commonly used during wartime. It saves the time of Parliament and enables a Government Department to make orders and regulations which have the force of law. Regulations of this kind have been common in local government circles for many years. Standards of service to be provided, procedure to be followed by a local authority in carrying out duties, fees to be charged, forms of documents and notices, and various other matters of detail are the kind of subject dealt with in such regulations.

Inspection by Government Departments. The function of the Ministry of Education in appointing inspectors to go round the country seeing if the schools and the instruction given in them are efficient is well known. It provides an example of a series of powers given to Government Departments to carry out inspections into the services provided by local authorities. Officers of the Ministry of Housing and Local Government may be authorized to attend meetings of district councils and take part in the proceedings but not vote. Police services, fire services, and public health services are subject to similar inspection by officers of the Central

Government. Housing and Planning inspectors are appointed to advise and assist local authorities in making and administering housing and town planning schemes. All these inspectors exercise a certain influence over the operations of the local councils. A favourable report by a government inspector is sometimes a necessary preliminary to the payment of a government grant.

General supervision. Certain Cabinet Ministers have been given by Parliament a direct duty of supervision over local services. For instance, the Minister of Health, when the appointment was first instituted in 1919, was given the duty of 'promoting the health of the people throughout England and Wales'. The Minister of Transport was given the function of improving 'the means of, and the facilities for, locomotion and transport'. The duty of the Minister of Education is 'to promote the education of the people of England and Wales, and the progressive development of institutions devoted to that purpose, and to secure the effective execution by local authorities under his control and direction, of the national policy for providing a varied and comprehensive educational service in every area'.

Such terms of appointment give the Minister in question a clear right and duty to interfere in local administration. But even when the appointment of the Minister has no such express terms it is a frequent practice for the Government Department concerned to interest itself in local matters. All Government Departments concerned with local services make it their business to send out to local authorities circulars giving advice, instructions how to proceed, explanations of Acts of Parliament and of regulations, and statistical and other information.

The Minister of Housing and Local Government and the Home Secretary have a general power to require all local authorities to send in reports and returns about their work. Other Government Departments have similar powers in respect of particular services.

When a local authority promotes a Bill in Parliament to obtain further powers it is always necessary that the Minister of Housing and Local Government should approve the Bill before it is proceeded with, and the Ministry, even after the Bill has gone forward, usually presents a report to Parliament on the merits of the proposals in the Bill.

Conferment and transfer of powers. The Minister of Housing and Local Government has power, within certain limits, to confer on a local authority powers not ordinarily possessed by that authority. He may, for instance, give a rural district council, in respect of a particular matter, powers equal to those of an urban district council. He may also, with the consent of the authorities concerned, transfer and rearrange powers as between the London County Council, the City of London Corporation, and the Metropolitan Borough Councils.

It will be seen, therefore, that in all the ways indicated above, the Central Government, through its Departments, can obtain considerable insight and oversight concerning the doings of local government authorities and the services they carry out. The influence and control of the Government Departments are, however, not the only methods by which local authorities may be subjected to control from above.

(B) JUDICIAL CONTROL

Local authorities are the creatures of the law. It will have been appreciated from what has been said in Chapter 4 that local government authorities are brought into existence and conditioned throughout their existence by the operation of law. Local authorities have no natural birth like a human being and no natural life or natural powers. They are the creations of man's own artifice. Whether created by a charter of incorporation, or by Act of Parliament, they are artificial entities and have only such existence, powers, and functions as the law confers.

The form and composition, the capacity and potentiality of a local authority cannot, like those of a human person, be measured by any natural standard. A local authority has no natural body. It is incorporated – that is, given a body – by operation of law; such bodily existence as is conferred upon it is just a legal conception. The extent of an authority's powers, the validity of its acts, the manner of performing its functions, all arise from the law and are laid down by law. Its activities are measurable only by legal standards. Accordingly, if a local authority does not act as it should, then it can be made answerable before the courts of law.

Duty of a local authority as a private person. Like other corporate bodies, like limited liability companies for instance, the artificial character of its creation limits the activities and consequently the legal responsibilities of a local authority. A 'body corporate' cannot walk or move about. Consequently it cannot commit an assault or burglary and cannot, as a body corporate, be imprisoned. But this does not mean to say that it is not subject to the ordinary law of the land, so far as the ordinary law can be made applicable. If a local authority fails to pay its taxes, refuses to meet its contracts or does some act which is contrary to the general law of the land, as by authorizing the issue of statements which are libellous, the local authority can be sued as if it were an ordinary person.

This liability is, of course, separate from, and in addition to, the individual liability of members and officers of a local authority for any illegal acts they do in the course of their duties.

Duty of a local authority to keep within its powers. In addition to being legally responsible as a private (although highly artificial) person, a local authority, because its whole existence is artificial, can only lawfully act at all within the framework given to it by the law. Just as a limited liability company can carry on only such business as is allowed by its memorandum of association, so a local authority can legally exercise only such powers as the law has conferred upon it. If it goes beyond these powers its acts will be *ultra vires* and accordingly unlawful.

The application of this general principle, the extent to which a local authority can be made answerable, the legal steps by which it can be brought to justice and the various ways in which the courts can impose remedies, penalties, and other punishment, and generally enforce the law in relation to local authorities are matters for legal specialists. It is not intended to go into the detailed technical refinements here. It may be of interest, however, to give a general outline of a very complicated subject.

Injury to private persons by public activities. The legal position of a local authority is complicated by the distinction between the *powers* of a local authority (things which the authority *may* do) and the *duties* of the authority (things which the authority is legally *obliged* to do).

Certain powers of local authorities are permissive, that is, the local authority is not bound to exercise the powers, but may do so if it wishes. So, if it does such things and does them badly or carelessly, it will be answerable to anyone who is adversely affected. But if the powers are mandatory, that is, if the authority is required by law to carry them out, or if the authority is expressly given power to do certain acts, e.g., to erect a sewage disposal works on a certain piece of land, and the local authority, in exercising the powers, causes damage to someone, and that person sues the local authority, the authority can claim in defence that the injurious act was required or expressly authorized to be done by law. Accordingly, in any lawsuits of this kind, it will be for the court to examine the powers and duties of the local authority, and to see whether in fact the authority was acting properly and within its duty.

There are cases where the Act of Parliament specially provides a remedy for injurious effects caused by the carrying out of a local authority's duty. Compensation claimable by an owner of property adversely affected by a town planning scheme is an example.

Statutory Appeals to the Courts. In many Acts of Parliament provision is made for appeal against an act of a local authority. Where, for instance, a local authority serves notice on an owner of property requiring him to carry out drainage or similar works, or where an authority has made an order requiring the demolition of a house which is insanitary or in a dangerous condition, or where a slum clearance or town planning scheme has been made which affects the rights of private owners, the law provides that the offended person may appeal to the courts. In minor cases the appeal lies to the magistrates, in other cases it may lie to the county court, in others to the High Court, according to the provisions of the Act in question.

Injury to private persons through failure to perform duties. A case may arise in which a private person is adversely affected, not by a careless or excessive exercise of the local authority's powers (misfeasance), but by neglect on the authority's part to carry out its public duties at all (nonfeasance). For instance, a local authority may fail to repair a public road properly and thus cause injury to a road user. In such a case the authority is as a rule not liable. But a number of exceptions to this principle have been developed. Much depends on the wording of the particular Act of Parliament under which the local authority's duty arises. Some acts make special provision for a remedy to be given to a private person who is damaged by a failure of the local authority. In other instances the courts have interpreted a particular Act of Parliament in such a way as to allow a private individual to obtain damages for personal loss caused by the local authority's neglect of its public duties.

Responsibility to the public at large. The Attorney-General, on behalf of the general public, may take legal proceedings against a local authority both for failure to carry out duties and for doing things for which there is no legal power. Proceedings may be by way of indictment (for wrongdoing or for failure to do right); by application to the courts for an order of mandamus (to order the authority to do what it ought); by application to the court for an injunction (to restrain the authority from going on with what it is doing or proposes to do); for a declaration by the court (to settle the rights of the case); for an order of prohibition (to prevent an authority from exceeding its functions when acting as a tribunal, e.g., for the grant of cinema and other licences); or by an order of certiorari (to bring into court a matter which the local authority has power to decide, but which could better be decided by a court).

To determine which of these technical procedures is applicable to any particular case is a matter for legal experts.

In many instances, although the proceedings are based on the responsibility of the local authority to the public as a whole, it is allowable for a private person, who has been particularly affected by the matters complained of, to be associated with the proceedings so as to be able to obtain whatever remedy the court may award.

Actions by local authorities. Although the law provides numerous opportunities by which local authorities may be brought to justice, the law does not leave local authorities themselves without a remedy in cases where injury to an authority has been done. Local authorities are empowered to take legal proceedings for the promotion or protection of the interests of the inhabitants in their areas. They can sue persons for breach of contract, and for injury done to the corporate authority's property, as well as for other acts and misdoings of other persons which affect the local authority. And they have power, by suing for penalties, to enforce compliance with requirements which they may lawfully make, for example, by-laws, conditions attached to licences, and other rules and regulations made by an authority under legal powers.

Local authorities may even sue one another, and often do, in order to obtain a clear decision of the courts as to rights or wrongs of a matter affecting them. Provision is, however, made in a number of Acts of Parliament for disputes between local authorities to be dealt with by referring the matter to a Government Department for decision.

Litigation as a guide. The decisions of the courts arrived at as a result of all the various forms of legal action referred to above have an effect wider than just settling the individual dispute involved in each case. Reports of the cases are either published in official law reports, or are set out in the various local government journals, reviews, and other papers circulating in the local government world. In the result, members and officers of local authorities obtain a guide as to the proper legal course to be followed in carrying out their public work.

(c) CONTROL BY MAJOR AUTHORITIES OVER
MINOR AUTHORITIES

Methods of control. County Councils have certain opportunities (already mentioned in this chapter) of taking action where another local authority is in default. County councils outside London have power to order (with the agreement of the district council) the simultaneous retirement of the members of a district council every three years (instead of one third annually), have power to arrange and alter the wards for the election of district councillors; and they may, in certain circumstances, dissolve a parish council and re-group parishes.

The exercise by borough and district councils of functions on behalf of a county council subject to conditions contained in a scheme of delegation has been referred to in chapter 4.

CHAPTER 9

WHICH WAY IS IT ALL GOING?

Former trends. The development of local government over the long period of its history shows certain definite trends. In early times, its concern was limited to matters of public order, military service, and the maintenance of public roads and bridges. Under Queen Elizabeth I its scope was enlarged by the institution of poor-relief administered by the parish organization; and the functions relating to the making-up of roads and the repair of bridges were enlarged and more clearly stated. During the 19th century local government was developed to deal with problems of public health, education, and police. Separate local bodies were at first created to deal with the individual services as they were instituted. Later these separate bodies were merged into authorities having functions in relation to a number of services. With the creation in 1888 of the county boroughs, the notion of an all-purpose local authority received its formal expression. The transfer of poor-law services to the county councils and county borough councils in 1930 still further simplified the pattern of local organization. By 1933 the development of the local government system had arrived at one of the peak periods in its history. The pattern was clearly defined, and the classes of authority among whom local government services were distributed were few in number.

Present trends. Since 1933 the comparatively simple pattern has been broken into, and a trend began to develop in which local services were being taken away from local authorities and administered either by the Central Government, or by some other type of body.

As the services run by local authorities have increased in number and importance, the problem of securing a high level of modern efficiency has also increased. Areas which may be suitable for ordinary governmental or social purposes may not be the best for the running of a public utility service. Indeed, the area which may be best for one service may not be the best for another type of service. Water supply and drainage, for instance, depend to a large extent for their efficient running on geographical considerations. Services such as passenger transport, police, and fire-brigades have to be related to the size and shape of the built-up areas to the needs of which it is largely the purpose of those services to minister. In the case of some particular services it has been thought appropriate that the country as a whole should be responsible for the running of part of those services rather than to let them remain entirely a local affair.

Illustrations of the trends which developed after 1933 can be obtained from the Acts of Parliament passed since that date. The Unemployment Act, 1934, created the Unemployment Assistance Board, a national body, to have the care of the able-bodied unemployed and their dependants in so far as they are not covered by the national unemployment insurance scheme. The effect of the Act was to take away from the public assistance authorities a large class of persons to whom relief was formerly given out of local rates. The Act was an expression of the view that the responsibility for unemployment is a national rather than a local affair. In 1940 the responsibility for the care of certain old age pensioners, formerly dealt with by local authorities by way of public assistance, was transferred to the Board, which is now called the National Assistance Board.

This trend of movement from local administration of poor-relief to central administration received a further impetus from the National Assistance Act, 1948, under which the Board distributes monetary benefits, and local authorities provide residential accommodation and local welfare. The time has accordingly arrived when poor relief, instituted as a parish service by Queen Elizabeth I, and reformed in the 19th century by the amalgamation of parishes into poor-law unions, and transferred later to county and county borough administration, has virtually ceased.

By the Trunk Roads Act, 1936, certain trunk roads outside London were taken away from local administration and placed under the responsibility of the Government. It was found to be unsatisfactory to let a national main road be repaired at the discretion of the number of small authorities through whose areas the roads run, especially when the local authorities themselves felt it to be unfair that they should have to bear the cost of maintaining roads which served national rather than local purposes.

The Fire Brigades Act, 1938, prepared the way for the regionalization of the fire brigade service, by enabling local authorities to combine and cooperate. The experience of the war made necessary the transfer of all fire brigades from local authorities to a National Fire Service. By the Fire Services Act, 1947, the brigades were transferred to county and county borough councils with power to form joint authorities.

The Education Act, 1944, had the effect of taking away from a number of minor local authorities certain education functions, and of transferring those functions to the councils of counties and county boroughs.

The Town Planning Act, 1947, provided that local planning functions should be performed by the councils of counties and county boroughs, whereas previously, outside London, the planning authorities in counties had been the councils of county districts.

Regionalism and nationalization. For the first few years or so after the second world war, there was thus a general movement towards larger areas for many services. In one or two cases, the area of administration became the country as a whole; in other cases the areas became bigger by the transfer of services from district authorities to county councils.

In other cases, several important services which had been managed in many areas by local authorities, namely, gas supply, electricity supply, and hospitals were transferred to national authorities for administration over wide areas by Regional or Area Boards. For water supply a number of joint authorities have been established with areas including those of several local authorities.

This trend towards the regional form of administration has had serious effects. It has not only denuded local authorities, especially the smaller authorities, of a number of important services, but it has (so it is alleged) made the administration of those services less intimate, and more remote from the citizen; for, although an authority with a large area and resources is better able to finance local services than an authority with a smaller area, the authority with a large area cannot (it is said) be so aware of local needs as can the authority with the smaller area.

Moreover, for hospitals, gas and electricity, it was considered unworkable to have locally elected bodies; for there would have been too many elections, and the citizen would have been bothered and bored. Accordingly the authorities for these services – the Regional and Area Boards – are appointed by the Central Government, with the result that the administration of these bodies is not democratic.

As a consequence of all this, a contrary trend has begun to develop towards the transfer of services from county to district administration. Delegation has been much talked of, and has found formal expression in the Education Act, 1944, and the Local Government Act, 1958, which provide for the delegation, as indicated in Chapter 4, of certain education, health and welfare functions from county councils to smaller authorities.

Areas and status. Since 1933 it has become apparent that it is not only the range of public services which has needed alteration; the places in which those services are provided have altered too. There have been shifts of population; villages have become towns; small towns have grown big enough to claim the status of county boroughs; while some of our ancient boroughs have either gradually declined or have not kept pace with the growth of other towns, and have thus become, by modern standards, little more than villages.

It has become evident that the system of local government must be adapted to suit the changing conditions. In 1945 a Local Government Boundary Commission was set up by the Central Government to adjust local government areas, but the Commission soon found that it could not go very far in altering areas without having power (which it did not possess) to consider alterations in the distribution of functions among local authorities. The Commission felt itself unable to continue, and was dissolved in 1949.

A great deal of discussion thereupon took place between the Government Departments and the representative associations of local authorities. These associations represent the various classes of authorities. There is a County Councils Association, an Association of Municipal Corporations, an Urban District Councils Association, a Rural District Councils Association a Metropolitan Boroughs Standing Joint Committee, and a National Association of Parish Councils. It has become an established practice for the Government Departments to discuss matters of local government with these bodies and to consult with them on proposals for changes in legislation on local government affairs.

In July, 1956, the Government, after prolonged discussion with the associations, published a white paper on the Area and Status of Local Authorities in England and Wales (Cmd. 9831) in which the conclusion was reached that there was no convincing case for radically re-shaping the existing form of local government; and that what was needed was to make improvements to bring the system up to date.

The Local Government Commissions. The Local Government Act, 1958, makes an attempt to deal with this problem. The provisions of Part I of the Act, relating to finance, have already been referred to in Chapter 7. Part II of the Act deals with the review of areas, and provides for the establishment of two Local Government Commissions, one for England and one for Wales, with the duty of reviewing the organization of local government, except in Greater London (for which a Royal Commission had already been set up). The two Local Government Commissions have power to recommend alterations of areas, the creation and abolition of counties and boroughs, the conversion of a non-county borough or urban district into a county borough, and the conversion of a county borough into a non-county borough.

In certain 'special review areas' which include the great conurbations of Tyneside, Merseyside, West Midlands, West Yorkshire, and South-East Lancashire, the Commission concerned is empowered to consider alterations, creations, conversions, and abolitions of county districts.

The Commissions are subject to the general direction of the Minister of Housing and Local Government. They must give public notice of their intention to hold a review, and, after the review, must make their proposals open to public inspection before submitting them to the Minister. After hearing any objections, the Minister may approve or modify the proposals and submit them to Parliament for confirmation.

County Reviews. In counties outside the 'special review areas' each county council must review the circumstances of the county districts within the county and make to the Minister proposals for such changes as appear to be desirable in the interests of effective and convenient local government. These proposals may include alteration of areas and status, the abolition or creation of districts and parishes, and the 'inclusion of a non-county borough in a rural district', thus reducing the borough to parish level.

Public notice of any proposals, and opportunity for objections will be given. The Minister, after considering any objections, may make an order giving effect to the proposals. This order does not require confirmation by Parliament. The Minister may direct a county council to undertake a subsequent review, and may, in certain cases, ask the appropriate Commission to do the review.

Creation of county boroughs. The two Local Government Commissions have power to suggest, among other matters, the alteration of boundaries as between counties and county boroughs, and the creation or abolition of county boroughs. These matters have long been the subject of controversy. When in 1888 county boroughs were first created, the minimum population required was 50,000. Today this status can normally be obtained only by a town of 100,000. To be a self-dependent local unit, providing all its own local government services, a town needs not only large resources, but also a population large enough to justify separate provision of services. The creation of a county borough involves a loss of area (and therefore of resources from rate income) of the adjoining county. The county loses to the county borough. County councils accordingly look askance at the growth of county boroughs.

Rateable values are higher in town areas. So, when a town within a county expands, the rateable value of that town increases, and so therefore does the rateable value of the county in which the town is situated. Thus the urban areas of a county help to pay for the county services in the rural parts of the county. If the town grows big enough to claim county borough status, this means that the county council is in prospect of losing a highly-rated urban area.

Much depends on the type of property which has arisen in the urban areas. High-class housing development brings high property values and a good rate revenue. The inhabitants of such property usually make few demands on the rates. They often do not send their children to the public elementary schools, and may not wish to avail themselves of the clinics or other rate-aided services. Moreover they, or most of them, pay their rates promptly. Housing estates of the working-class type are, on the other hand, of comparatively low rateable value, but necessitate the provision of the whole range of public services. Considerations such as these often have a very real effect on the willingness or hesitancy of local authorities to take over or part with areas where urban development has taken place.

Extension of county boroughs. Somewhat similar problems arise when existing county boroughs get bigger. Suburbs spring up around them, and the urban development over-flows the administrative boundary of the original borough area. The citizen, going about his daily affairs, notices no visible boundary in fact between the borough and its over-flow. The inhabitants of the near suburbs feel themselves to be part of the original town. Many of them may be former residents of the old town, and still come into the town for their daily work, shopping, or entertainment. They demand the same local services as the town itself. There is often a delay in meeting this demand. The local government authority by which the suburbs are administered is not the same authority as that administering the borough. The outside authority may be relatively poor, and be unwilling to incur huge capital expenditure in fitting out these new suburbs with the range of expensive services until the rate income from the urban development begins to come in. Rates do not become payable until property is occupied. Accordingly the outside local authority will hesitate to provide services until the suburbs are already inhabited. A man who has moved out of the old town and bought a house in a newly developed suburb may at first find little there in the way of public services – no schools, no clinics, no public library. Naturally he grumbles. The authorities of the old town sympathize, especially if the new suburb consists of council houses erected by the borough council itself.

Accordingly claims arise for the extension of the area of the county borough so as to include the new suburbs. Such extensions have much to justify them. To extend the existing services of the town, the sewerage system, for instance, into the suburbs may often be cheaper than the provision of entirely new services by the outside local authority, and if the borough authorities are promoting urban development in the suburbs as, for instance, by the erection of a housing estate, the borough authority may be able to arrange to provide the local government services without waiting for the rate revenue from the housing estate to come in. Thus the time-lag in the provision of services can be avoided.

Formerly the creation or extension of a county borough could be obtained by promoting a Bill in Parliament. Until 1973, this procedure must not be adopted; the appropriate Local Government Commission must deal with the matter first.

Non-county boroughs. Reduction in status. Throughout the country there are a number of small boroughs, some of them very ancient, which have either failed to grow, or have declined in size. Some have populations under 2000, and have a rateable value so small that a penny rate yields less than £50. Such a borough finds it difficult to provide the range and standard of services of the normal borough.

A great deal of respect none the less attaches to the title and status of a borough. Accordingly, the Local Government Act, 1958, contains ingenious provisions to deal with these tiny boroughs so as to relieve them of some of their local government responsibility without depriving them entirely of their titles and dignity. The appropriate Commission or county council, in making review of the local government arrangements, may propose that a small non-county borough be included in a rural district. When a borough is so included, it will virtually become a parish, but it will not lose its charter, its borough name and title, or its mayor. It will, however, lose its aldermen. It will be known as a 'rural borough'. Its council will be, in effect, a parish council, although its members will be known as 'rural borough councillors'.

The public duty. The proposals which will emerge from

215

the activities of the Royal Commissions and from the various county reviews will doubtless lead to changes which will affect individual local authorities very much. Some authorities will cease to exist and their areas will be merged in other areas; some authorities may go up or go down in status; new authorities may come into being. These effects will not change the general structure or the general form and functioning of local government.

No Government is likely to abandon entirely a system of local government which has, during the past hundred years, helped to confer upon this country the civilizing influence of modern public services and has enabled local authorities to share with the Central Government the responsibility and the cost, as well as the pride, of that achievement.

There will always be need of a local government system – for bodies with local experience and intimate knowledge of local conditions to share with the Central Government the work of running this country. The whole country cannot be run entirely from Whitehall. There will still be a great need for public-spirited men and women to take part in the work of managing the local services, and there will still be great need for electors of all ages and classes to have a live and continuous interest in local government affairs.

Apathy at elections is the virtual death of democracy. If few electors vote, power gets into the hands of the few, and those few quickly get exposed to the temptations of self-sufficiency and slackness. Some people excuse their own apathy by the statement that local areas are too small, and that the affairs of local authorities savour of the parish pump. There is, however, no clear evidence to prove that electors in small areas are any less or any more enthusiastic than those in large areas. Some observers regard the parish as the vital unit in local government, others regard the county or the county borough as the only unit capable of stimulating public interest in any substantial degree. You can take which view you like, and you will find here and there an example to support whatever view you take. Conditions vary in each locality.

Local government is entering upon another transition stage. It is in periods of growth that the greatest watchfulness is required. Local government affects everyone. Every person in this country over 21 now has a local government vote, and therefore has a concern in the operations of his or her local authority. The vote is a privilege which carries with it a duty.

INDEX

Acceptance of office, 77
Accounts, 189
Actions by or against local authorities, 203 ff.
Adoptive Acts, 89
Aldermen, 60, 65, 78–9, 121
Allotments, 111
Areas, adaptation of, 14, 25
    alterations of, 49, 50, 52
Assigned revenues, 178
Associations of local authorities, 211
Audit, 190–2

Baths and wash-houses, 97–8
Births, deaths, and marriages, 112
Blind persons, 100
Borough, 29, 34, 43
    County, see County Borough
    freedom of, 43
    Metropolitan, see Metropolitan Borough
    Non-County, see Non-County Borough
Borrowing, 169, 186
Boundaries, alteration of, 50, 51
Bridges, 108–9
Building, control of, 102
Burial, 111
By-laws, 112

Certiorari, 34, 203
Chairman, 63 ff., 78
Charter, 29, 32, 51, 85

Cinemas, 110
City, 44
City of London, 54–6, 82, 117, 163
City Manager, 21, 130
Civil Service, 155, 166
Clerk of a local authority, 146, 156
Commissioners, 20, 35
Commissions of the Peace, 45–6
Committees, 119 ff.
    meetings of, 136 ff.
    of Parliament, 120
Conditions of service, 149
Constable, 26, 28
Control, central, 32, 193 ff.
    judicial, 33, 199 ff.
Coroner, 27
Corporation, 44
    close, 30
Corrupt practices, 74
Council, size of, 66
County, 24, 38, 45
    administrative, 37, 46, 50
    area, 25, 50
    courts, 25, 41
    palatine, 29
County Borough, 37, 48
    creation of, 48
    extension of, 49
    powers, 114
County Council, 38, 46, 50, 52
    powers, 115
Courts, freemen's county, 25
    hundred, 24, 26
    leet, 28
Courts of Justice, 41, 45

Deputy chairman, 64
Deputy mayor, 63
Disease, 97
Disqualification for election, 79 ff.
Duchy, 29

Education, 37, 104–6, 208
Education officer or director, 160
Election of aldermen, 78–9
Election of chairman or mayor, 78
  of councillors, mode of, 68
  expenses, 73
  qualification for, 67
Electoral areas, 50–1, 52, 54, 56
  registration, 68 ff.
Employment agencies, 110
Entertainments licensing, 110
Estimates, 187

Fertilizers and feeding stuffs, 110
Feudal system, 23
Finance procedure, 187
  in the future, 207 ff.
Financial officer, 160
Fire brigades, 110, 207
Food and drugs, 96–7
Foreign systems of local government, 20
Franchise, 29
  electoral, see Elections
Frankpledge, 22, 26, 28

Government control, 193 ff.
  grants, 169, 177 ff.

Health, see Public Health
Highways, 30, 35, 96, 106 ff, 208
Honour (area), 28

Hospitals, 99, 209
Housing, 100
  grants, 184
Hundred, 24

Joint Boards and Committees,
  58–9, 93
Judicial control, 33, 199 ff.
Justice, administration of, 15, 41,
  46
Justices of the Peace, 26, 31, 32, 41

Land charges, 112
Lathes, 24
Legal position of local authorities,
  199 ff.
Liberty (area), 28
Libraries, 109
Licensing, entertainments, 110
  liquor, 41 ff.
  music and dancing, 42, 110
Local government,
  development of, 13, 30, 206
  Elizabethan, 30
  foreign, 20
  future trends, 206
  in the 18th century, 33
  in the 19th century, 36
  London, 34, 56
  meaning of, 15
  medieval, 14, 22
  organization of, 126
  pattern of, 47–8
  practical working of, 119
  purpose of, 16, 113
  value of, 18, 113
Local Government Board, 37

Local services, 15, 16
  mode of providing, 17
Lodging houses, 103
London, 34, 37, 44, 54–6, 82, 117–18, 163
London Transport Executive, 57
Lord Lieutenant, 27

Manor, 23
Maternity and child welfare, 98, 131
Mayor, 61, 63, 78, 82
Medical officer, 146, 148, 150, 157
Meetings, 82, 136–8
Members, expenses of, 143
  qualification for election, 67
  salaries for, 150
  term of office, 64
  work of, 131–2, 143–4
Metropolitan Borough Council, 37, 44, 57, 117
Metropolitan Water Board, 40, 57
Midwives, 98
Ministerial control, 194 ff.
Ministry of Health, 37
Motor vehicles licensing, 112, 184
Music and dancing, 42, 110

New York, 20
Non-County Borough, 51
  powers, 115
Nuisances, 96
Nursing homes, 100

Offensive trades, 96
Officers of local authorities, 146 ff.
Open spaces, 104
Overcrowding, 102

Palatine, county, 23, 31, 37, 52 ff., 116
Parks, 104
Parliament, 113
  committees of, 120
Pecuniary interest of
  members, 141
  officers, 163
Pensions, 153–4
Petrol, 111
Police, 46, 49, 109
Politics in local government, 139–41
Poor relief, 30, 35, 36, 38, 106, 208
Port of London Authority, 57
Powers of local authorities, 85 ff.
  transfer of, 90
Precepts, 175
Private Acts, 88
Prohibition, writ of, 34, 203
Public health, 36, 94
Public utility services, 39 ff., 111

Quarter sessions, 26, 31, 41

Rapes, 24
Rates, 31, 35, 169 ff.
Refuse collection, 96
Regionalism, 209
Roads, see Highways, 106–8
Rural District Council, 38, 54, 116

Sanitary areas, 37
Sewers and drains, 94–5
Sheriff, 25
Shops, 111

Slum clearance, 101
Soke, 28
Star Chamber, 32
Surveyor, 159

Term of office, 64
Thames Conservators, 57
Theatres, 110
Tithing, 22
Town Clerk, 146, 156
Town planning, 103
Township, 22
Treasurer, 160

Unemployment, 207
Urban District Council, 38, 48, 52
   powers, 116
U.S.A., 20

Vaccination, 97
Vestry, 24, 30, 54
Vill, 22
Voting, at meetings, 137 ff.
   qualification for, 69

Wapentakes, 24
Water, 95
Weights and Measures, 111